# THROUGH THEIR EYES

## INTO THE UNKNOWN

Edited By Lynsey Evans

First published in Great Britain in 2024 by:

Young Writers
Remus House
Coltsfoot Drive
Peterborough
PE2 9BF
Telephone: 01733 890066
Website: www.youngwriters.co.uk

All Rights Reserved
Book Design by Ashley Janson
© Copyright Contributors 2024
Softback ISBN 978-1-83565-524-5
Printed and bound in the UK by BookPrintingUK
Website: www.bookprintinguk.com
YB0593D

# FOREWORD

Since 1991, here at Young Writers we have celebrated the awesome power of creative writing, especially in young adults, where it can serve as a vital method of expressing strong (and sometimes difficult) emotions, a conduit to develop empathy, and a safe, non-judgemental place to explore one's own place in the world. With every poem we see the effort and thought that each pupil published in this book has put into their work and by creating this anthology we hope to encourage them further with the ultimate goal of sparking a life-long love of writing.

*Through Their Eyes* challenged young writers to open their minds and pen bold, powerful poems from the points-of-view of any person or concept they could imagine – from celebrities and politicians to animals and inanimate objects, or even just to give us a glimpse of the world as they experience it. The result is this fierce collection of poetry that by turns questions injustice, imagines the innermost thoughts of influential figures or simply has fun.

The nature of the topic means that contentious or controversial figures may have been chosen as the narrators, and as such some poems may contain views or thoughts that, although may represent those of the person being written about, by no means reflect the opinions or feelings of either the author or us here at Young Writers.

We encourage young writers to express themselves and address subjects that matter to them, which sometimes means writing about sensitive or difficult topics. If you have been affected by any issues raised in this book, details on where to find help can be found at
*www.youngwriters.co.uk/info/other/contact-lines*

# CONTENTS

## Bryn Celynnog Comprehensive School, Beddau

| | |
|---|---|
| William Sturcbecher (12) | 1 |
| Angaleena Deepu (12) | 2 |
| Jeffin Jibu (12) | 3 |

## Christ's School, Richmond

| | |
|---|---|
| Israela Adeyoju (13) | 4 |
| Pablo Phillips (18) | 5 |
| Abigail Harris (12) | 6 |
| Sophie Greatholder (16) | 7 |
| Bilal Shahid Qazi | 8 |

## Cottingham High School, Cottingham

| | |
|---|---|
| Adam El-Homsi (11) | 9 |
| Riley Watkins (12) | 10 |
| Evie Dunn (14) | 12 |
| Yvie Bush (12) | 14 |
| Melissa Anderson (13) | 16 |
| Caleb Ramsey (13) | 18 |
| Ava Robinson (12) | 20 |
| Iyesha Wilson (13) | 22 |
| Eliza Mann-Berue (12) | 24 |
| Samuel Hodgson (13) | 26 |
| Noah Watkins (12) | 28 |
| Jessica Danyi (13) | 30 |
| Will Grady (13) | 32 |
| Jack Butler (13) | 33 |
| Alice Dobbs (12) | 34 |
| Louisa Shepherdson (13) | 35 |
| Max Wilson (12) | 36 |
| Matilda Keane (12) | 37 |

| | |
|---|---|
| James Nalson (11) | 38 |
| Mason Edmond (11) | 39 |
| Zak Robinson (14) | 40 |
| Frances Young (13) | 41 |
| Lily Cook (12) | 42 |
| Robert Roper (12) | 43 |

## Eltham Hill School, Eltham Hill

| | |
|---|---|
| Freya Davies (15) | 44 |

## Fleetwood High School, Fleetwood

| | |
|---|---|
| Harley Johnstone (12) | 45 |
| Lily Hesketh (15) | 46 |
| Gracie Leddy (11) | 49 |
| Thomas Cameron (12) | 50 |
| Hallie Butler (12) | 52 |
| Eleanor Cox (12) | 53 |
| Lily Holden (15) | 54 |
| Alex Pook (12) | 56 |
| Christopher Pochin (11) | 57 |
| Lacie Atkin (11) | 58 |
| Louisa Beech (11) | 59 |
| Jake Warburton (12) | 60 |
| Belle Martin (11) | 61 |
| Lexi-Leigh MacDonald (12) | 62 |
| Daniel Dadson (12) | 63 |
| Lilly-Mai Walker (12) | 64 |
| Nadia Salthouse (12) | 65 |
| Simon Shaw (12) | 66 |
| Star Elliott (11) | 67 |
| Pixie-lee Tavernor (11) | 68 |
| Lexi Rees (12) | 69 |
| Tiffany Tseneva (12) | 70 |
| Samuel Newton (12) | 71 |

| | |
|---|---|
| Lexi Myerscough (11) | 72 |
| Isabelle Lloyd (12) | 73 |
| Evelyn Clough (11) | 74 |
| Skye Taylor (12) | 75 |
| Daisy Kelly-Rutherford (12) | 76 |
| Amelia Calligan (11) | 77 |
| Megan Morrissey (12) | 78 |
| Mollie Wood (12) | 79 |
| Yoshi Robson (12) | 80 |
| Alfie Morgan (12) | 81 |
| Katie Balmer (12) | 82 |
| Jaidan Lyall (12) | 83 |
| Layla Fuller (12) | 84 |
| Alfie Brown (11) | 85 |
| Lily Willacy-Dodd (11) | 86 |
| Kyle Dewett (12) | 87 |
| Poppy Howell (11) | 88 |
| Alfie Stanley (12) | 89 |
| Lillie Hatcher (12) | 90 |
| Pippa Wilson (12) | 91 |
| Sonny Prior (11) | 92 |
| Oscar Dudley (11) | 93 |
| Ryan Jennison (11) | 94 |
| Jack Roberts (11) | 95 |
| Lilly-Jayne Morton (12) | 96 |
| Tyler Pendlebury (11) | 97 |
| Peter Smith (11) | 98 |
| Troy Stott (12) | 99 |
| Alexander Hill (12) | 100 |
| Alexus Kennedy (11) | 101 |
| Tiarna Quinn (12) | 102 |
| Lucy Rayworth (12) | 103 |
| Elliot Rees (12) | 104 |
| Darcy Hone (12) | 105 |
| Millie Abram (12) | 106 |
| Delilah Lamb (11) | 107 |

## Fulston Manor School, Sittingbourne

| | |
|---|---|
| Evie Chantler-Harris (12) | 108 |
| Megan Fulton (11) | 110 |
| Sophia Seal (13) | 112 |
| Jacob Nanson (12) | 114 |

## Gartree High School, Oadby

| | |
|---|---|
| Rhys Hannam (13) | 115 |

## Nicholas Breakspear Catholic School, St Albans

| | |
|---|---|
| Christine Oguno (12) | 116 |
| Oliver Richardson (14) | 117 |
| James Lochmuller (12) | 118 |
| N'rai Dorsett-Johnson (12) | 120 |
| Ryan Todd (12) | 122 |
| Daisy Morgan O'Grady (12) | 123 |
| Skye Minnette (13) | 124 |
| Chukwuemeka Ogashi (11) | 125 |
| Lucy Hamilton (11) | 126 |
| Nicola Pistoia (12) | 127 |
| Daniel Harris (12) | 128 |
| Cameron Mitchell (12) | 129 |
| Tilly Durack Lawlor (11) | 130 |
| Poppy Saunders (13) | 131 |
| Domenico Di Bella (11) | 132 |
| Grace Curry (12) | 133 |
| Chigozirim Okoh (11) | 134 |
| Alexandru Ghitan (14) | 135 |
| Finn Flatley (12) | 136 |
| Cecilia Turton-Ryz (12) | 137 |
| Harry Mcmahon (12) | 138 |
| Angelo Grafanakis (13) | 139 |
| Kenisha Rebello (14) | 140 |
| Beatrice Lyden (13) | 141 |
| George Marron-Porter (11) | 142 |
| Caroline Antwi (11) | 143 |
| Harry Brandon Mukesha (14) | 144 |
| Gilda Kyeremeh (13) | 145 |
| Hannah Guerrini (13) | 146 |
| Holly Vanderhoven (12) | 147 |
| Salman Taman (13) | 148 |
| Natalia Di Girgenti (12) | 149 |
| Erik Verboom (11) | 150 |
| Pippa Mann (11) | 151 |
| Michael Ojo (11) | 152 |
| Oliver Bradshaw (14) | 153 |
| Marcel Giorko (11) | 154 |

| | |
|---|---|
| Michael Oliver (12) | 155 |
| Heidi Rouse (11) | 156 |
| Eric Balan (13) | 157 |
| Ollie Brandle (14) | 158 |
| Mia Lamptey (11) | 159 |
| Jakub Ostrowski (14) | 160 |
| Alexander Mazoruk (13) | 161 |
| Charlie Burns (11) | 162 |
| Ruairí Hickey (13) | 163 |
| Ellie Davies (11) | 164 |
| Pulane Urneh (13) | 165 |
| Ruby Martin (12) | 166 |
| Erin Dunnigan (12) | 167 |
| Nathaniel Hettiarachchi (14) | 168 |
| Niall Hubbard (11) | 169 |
| Ryan Shine (13) | 170 |
| Francesca Avila (11) | 171 |

## Poole High School, Poole

| | |
|---|---|
| Lily Dauncey (13) | 172 |
| Erin Harker (12) | 173 |
| Olivia Young (13) | 174 |
| Jasmine Dodgson (12) | 175 |
| Aaron King (12) | 176 |

## Queen Mary's College, Basingstoke

| | |
|---|---|
| Reo Warwick (16) | 177 |

## Rainey Endowed School, Magherafelt

| | |
|---|---|
| Henry Haddock (16) | 179 |

## Roundhill Academy, Thurmaston

| | |
|---|---|
| Tillie Orton (12) | 180 |
| Manjot Singh (12) | 181 |
| Maya Patel (11) | 182 |
| Charlie Bailey (12) | 183 |
| Isla-Mae Simpson (11) | 184 |
| Emma Limb (11) | 185 |
| Asha Lakhani (11) | 186 |
| Anika Khushalbhai (12) | 187 |

| | |
|---|---|
| Keelan Brown (11) | 188 |
| Connie McDonald (11) | 189 |
| Kyle Smith (12) | 190 |
| Mia Brookes (12) | 191 |
| Brooke Simmons (12) | 192 |
| Rikin Thanki (11) | 193 |

## Stopsley High School, Luton

| | |
|---|---|
| Serena Ayube (13) | 194 |

## Swanwick Hall School, Alfreton

| | |
|---|---|
| Lilley-Mae Ryn-Wild (12) | 196 |

## The Heys School, Prestwich

| | |
|---|---|
| Mergen Ariunzol (11) | 197 |
| Nate Sloan (12) | 198 |
| Nnenna Okocha (11) | 200 |

## The Peterborough School, Peterborough

| | |
|---|---|
| Jack Rigby (15) | 201 |

## The Salesian Academy Of St John Bosco, Bootle

| | |
|---|---|
| Princess Adora Aiyeki Uyinmwen (15) | 203 |
| Jay Keir (12) | 204 |
| Leticia Frozi Bona (13) | 205 |
| Charlie Mullin (12) | 206 |
| Marie Didiova (12) | 207 |
| Isabella Flynn-Farley (12) | 208 |
| Jack Mullin (12) | 209 |
| Fiona Raduta (12) | 210 |
| Caitlyn Bailey (14) | 211 |
| Ava Brady (13) | 212 |
| Lily Grace Richman | 213 |
| Analishia Hessing McGinn (12) | 214 |
| Declan Parker (14) | 215 |
| Lily Benton Newman (12) | 216 |
| Tyler Draper (12) | 217 |

| | |
|---|---|
| Laila McDonough (12) | 218 |
| Mylie Walsh (12) | 219 |
| Emilee Stevens (12) | 220 |
| Mary Robinson (15) | 221 |
| Caiden Molloy (13) | 222 |
| Carmen Roscoe (13) | 223 |
| Emma-Jayne Smith (15) | 224 |
| Thomas Meath (12) | 225 |
| Sophie Duckworth (14) | 226 |
| Jessica O'Brien (12) | 227 |
| Luca Vincent | 228 |
| Chloe Williams (13) | 229 |

**Uddingston Grammar School, Uddingston**

| | |
|---|---|
| Kacey Brown (13) | 230 |

# THE POEMS

# The Minotaur

I was a gift
Supposed to be sacrificed
But due to my beauty
I was kept as a prize.

This enraged a god
Whose anger cursed my soul
Turned me into a beast
A beast who craved human flesh.

I was out of control
And the labyrinth was built
The head of a bull
And the body of a man.

I was imprisoned inside
A maze of many parts
All day I roam
Seeing through the darkness
At the centre I call home
Through no fault of my own.

## William Sturcbecher (12)
Bryn Celynnog Comprehensive School, Beddau

# School Library

There is a library in my school,
That quiet, people used to go,
Choose a spot that's comfortable,
And you can simply read,
Enjoy your book,
Take your time,
Don't read for speed,
When you are finished,
You know what to do next,
Put your book away,
In a proper place,
Keep our library clean,
It's our favourite place.

## Angaleena Deepu (12)
Bryn Celynnog Comprehensive School, Beddau

# Beauty Of Wales

Land of dragons and misty hills
Wales where nature weaves its spell
Castells echo tales untold
Songs of bards, ancient and bold
Cymru's beauty, a story to unfold.

**Jeffin Jibu (12)**
Bryn Celynnog Comprehensive School, Beddau

# Where The Tide Meets The Land

The waves shimmer within my eyes,
The tide says its final goodbyes,
The wind sings its beautiful songs,
Like a siren, its lullaby goes on.

A lifeless stick drifts closer,
The twig touches the composer,
It's pulled and flung through the air,
Landing on the gleaming sand oh so bare.

A red creature of hope rises from the ground,
This little stick never having its own sound,
Unlike his kin boats or ships,
His future like a meteor plummets and dips.

But the red creature of hope began to climb,
Looked at its body not worth a dime,
The red gleam of hope wanted it as its own,
Even if it was as tiny as a black gull's bone.

The stick was needed in a vital role,
Even though compared to his brother he was like a doll,
It was still as important for it to do its part,
Even though doubts and troubles eventually may start.

We all may need that extra kick,
Just like the crab needed its little stick.

**Israela Adeyoju (13)**
Christ's School, Richmond

# Look At Me Before You Cry

Look at me before you cry,
I deserve the pain behind your eyes,
Willows watched as blue skies turned cold,
And the velvet grass fell withered and old,
On the day I knew your heart had died.

Sing to me before you leave,
Your voice was always young and free,
Winds did chime as you sang so sweet,
Of the time we had which you felt would fleet,
On the day I knew you had left my side.

So turn and face me one last time,
And yet it's been years since I felt you as mine,
So now I sit, admiring the past,
In this field once loved, now hollowed glass,
Waiting for your light to return as my guide.

And although the silence has swallowed your cry,
I can still see the pain that's behind your eyes.

## Pablo Phillips (18)
Christ's School, Richmond

# My Wait For Freedom

I have sat here alone for too long,
Awaiting my unfortunate fate,
I don't know what will happen to me, but I try to stay hopeful,
I'm not important enough to be saved.

I don't have a special family name or tie,
I was an ordinary citizen, who was only doing what was right,
And yet I still sit here in my sea of pity for myself, and wait,
Waiting for my day, my chance, my future of being free.

I only wait to hear that my loved ones are safe,
I wait to be told war is over,
I wait to hear that I can go home.
But I am waiting, listening anxiously for my moment,
My chance to be free.

## Abigail Harris (12)
Christ's School, Richmond

# Sky Rats

Now you may see a feral friend,
Or pest who'll meet a grisly end,
But once we were your greatest pride,
When racing birds would soar and glide
Through empty skies of ancient lands,
Over white cliffs and desert sands.
But long gone are our days of grace,
And now we seem a waste of space,
As eyes dart around Trafalgar Square,
I beat my wings through the city air.
If there is a God above,
He would have had me born a dove.
So now's the time to give a smidgen
Of respect to the bird we call the pigeon.

**Sophie Greatholder (16)**
Christ's School, Richmond

# Flight Of The Godwit

Wings burning,
Begging for mercy,
Destination calls,
Forget controversy.

Look forward,
Ignore the pain,
Lay the eggs,
Do it all again.

Look for land,
And land, you must,
Make your nest,
In god we trust.

Fledglings cry,
Turn your back,
As you fly,
From where you came.

**Bilal Shahid Qazi**
Christ's School, Richmond

# The Silenced

*This poem shows the negatives and positives that are placed upon mankind from faith*

As religion takes domination,
Oh, how could it be possible to create such an abomination?
As day by day, arrows would grasp on the disbelievers,
Yet they won't ever know religion is something much, much deeper.

Words are twisted like how the arrow flies,
Yet many are punished for daring to ask why.
Nobody knows and certainly nobody cares,
About why the world is so unfair.

The blood from their hands may stain,
But how will it forgive all the victims' pain?
Blood can be washed off with just water,
How is it that easy to cause a mass slaughter?

Why can't one day, they all agree
To let the victims be eternally free,
It's depressing to know it's done for others' pleasure,
Even though the believers have to go through so much pressure.

If the world could just all unite,
Oh, how many would stop the fights,
If the world could clean all of its blood,
It certainly, certainly should.

## Adam El-Homsi (11)
Cottingham High School, Cottingham

# Zeus' Greek Gods

Ares, god of war and courage, son of Zeus, and one of the twelve Olympians;
Boreas, god of the cold north wind, and bringer of winter;
Chaos, filled the gap between heaven and earth, created the first beings;
Dionysus, Olympian god of the grape harvest, winemaking and wine;
Erubus, primordial god of darkness.

Few have been chosen, and more still to go,
this team of the greatest gods will scare any foe.

Glaucus ate a magic herb and became immortal, a god of the sea;
Hades, king of the underworld, god of deeds and riches;
Iapetus, god of mortality, helped restrain Urcaus and became the western pillar that helped hold up the sky.

Joining these mighty gods to make Zeus' team some of the best, we can but dream.

Kratos, god of power and strength;
Lelantos, god of air, moving unseen and a hunter's skill at stalking;
Morpheus, god of sleep and dreams with the skill to influence the dreams of gods and kings;
Nereus, Titan god of sea before Poseiden, father of the nymphs of the sea;
Oceanus, Titan god of the ocean, personifies the world ocean, enormous river encircling the world;

Poseidon, Oympian, new god of the sea, earthquakes, storms and horses.

Quite a collection Zeus' team now makes,
a few more to go before he puts on the brakes.

Rhadamanthus, King of Ocalea, and judge of the dead, son of Zeus;
Selene, Titan goddess of the moon, grandchild of Gaia and Uranus;
Tartarus, god of the deep abyss, a great pit in the depths of the underworld;
Uranus, primordial god of the sky and heavens, father of the Titans.

Victory will come when this team work together;
Wonders of the Greek, helpers and protectors, punishers of the unjust;
Expect the best, this team will deliver;
You can put your faith in the Greek gods, that is a must!

Zeus, king of the gods and father of gods and men, leads through immortality, the greatest team of all time.

## Riley Watkins (12)
Cottingham High School, Cottingham

# Rooted To The Ground

Poison ivy climbs up my lungs,
Using my rib cage as a trellis.
I choke on the roots that tangle in my throat,
They grow into a natural stutter,
Not worth watering.
Stem and orchid pierce my arteries,
Whilst vines wrap my heart.
Potential decays in my veins,
Rotten roots writhe in my gut,
Spilling globules of pearly red.

The axe came clumsily, with a graceless swing,
They would be sorry when there was none of us left.

We wished of dying with dignity,
Hundred-year-old trees crashing down with honour,
Branches splitting gracefully,
Trunks collapsing as a martyr on the battlefield,
Heart in wood splinters, but that was not this.

It's not that I wouldn't have minded
The careless treading of my flowers
If they had been beautifully violent,
I would never have forgiven the destruction,
But the gracelessness of the axe's swing
Made my flowers recoil.

They brought with them axe and fire,
And with them came fuel and flame,
Woodcutters and axemen.
They wandered through my forest,
Clumsily hacking at hundred-year-old wood.
That graceless lumbering,
That awkward blundering.

I watched them strip this forest of trees,
I was next.

Plants spray across my body like wet paint
Thrown to a wall, sleeping in every corner.
A young couple carve their initials into my flesh,
I watch bright buds that never bloom,
I watch bulbs that rot in the soil,
Sowing seeds of doubt in my mind.
I peel back layers of decay,
Splitting my own ribs open like a wooden chest,
To show these axemen,
Even trees have more heart than them.

My roots are tangled to the woodland floor,
I lie still, moss covers me in a soft green decay.
I was too vulnerable to your graceless axe,
I could not run.

## Evie Dunn (14)
Cottingham High School, Cottingham

# Life As A Teen

I wake up, thinking it's still the school holidays,
I hear bustling in the kitchen downstairs,
In that moment, I realise it is the first day back at school,
No way, I am going to be late,
"Mum, where's my tie?" As I leap out of bed,
Shower, teeth, breakfast, drink,
So little time, I cannot think,
Oh no, I'm going to be late,
Something I really hate,
I get there ten minutes behind,
Detention for me, I'm convinced,
What are they like?
I have never had anything like that before,
Will I ever be in more trouble than I am in?
What should I do?

Teachers nagging at me to pick my options,
How am I supposed to know, I'm only a child?
Too much pressure with all this,
It's messing with my head, Miss,
I don't like how the other kids are,
Getting a designer coat won't get me far,
I don't need to fit in or conform,
I get reminded it is parents' evening,
It felt like a lifetime in the cell, waiting for my mum,
Wondering what my teachers were going to say,

Getting told I was predicted grade threes,
I wanted grade nines,
Silence in the car,
No sound is heard.

Back to my room for studying,
Books stacked up as tall as me,
Get on my phone to see a message,
Getting cyberbullied for, well, nothing,
Seriously, my stomach is aching,
It's too much stress for me,
But it's a day in the life of a year nine student.

## Yvie Bush (12)
Cottingham High School, Cottingham

# Dreamscape

In the hand of the artist, I come alive,
With bristles soft, yet strong to strive.
To bring life to canvas, colours to blend,
In the world of imagination, I have no end.

I dance across the surface, a stroke of delight,
Creating beauty with each careful flight,
From vivid hues to subtle shades,
I am the tool by which art is made.

With each dip in paint, I carry the dream
Of the one who holds me, their creative stream.
I am the messenger of their vision and skills,
Capturing moments, emotions, thrills.

I am a humble tool, but in the right hand,
I become something more, a masterpiece grand,
So I will continue to work, to create and blend,
Until the final artwork is complete in the end.

I am the conduit of the artist's soul,
Translating their thoughts, making them whole.
I sweep across the canvas with purpose and grace,
Capturing the world in this small space.

With every stroke, I tell a story,
Of love, of loss, of joy and glory.
I am the brush that breathes life into art,
A silent partner, playing my part.

I bear witness to the artist's mood,
As they pour their heart into every hue,
With each dab and swirl, I am their guide,
Creating a masterpiece, side by side.

So I will continue to dance and create,
To bring their vision to life, to never abate.

**Melissa Anderson (13)**
Cottingham High School, Cottingham

# Silent Reverie

In my sanctuary room, I find my own cocoon,
Wrapped in solitude, as if beneath a crescent moon,
Gaming through the hours, a refuge to consume,
Especially in the blossoming days of May's perfume.

My mental state, a turbulent sea, a frown it wears,
A lonely canvas painted with my unspoken cares,
Venturing under the sun's embrace, no joy appears,
In the world's grand theatre, I'm lost in my own fears.

Society's rhythm, a dissonant din, we strive to understand,
Caught in a paradox, can't grasp its shifting sand,
Constantly tethered to our phones, in a digital land,
A solitary dance, an unseen hand.

Messages transmitted, conversations delayed,
A metre apart, yet the connection frayed,
Can't we break free from this technological raid,
And step into the sunlight, where memories are made?

Yet my hesitant mind resists, urges me to stay,
In the quiet realm, where thoughts find their way,
Respect these musings, like a delicate ballet,
In the solitude, where I choose to sway.

Alone, not lonely,
In the depths of my own zone,
A symphony of thoughts,
A space to call my own.

**Caleb Ramsey (13)**
Cottingham High School, Cottingham

# War And Peace

It started off as a thought that crossed our minds,
A thought that slightly discomforted us,
A fearful notion of dispute and conflict,
That was overlooked by too many people,
We were repeatedly warned,
Until it was too late.

First, the attack, then the struggle,
It felt unreal in a way that left a feeling of dread and despair,
Appalling things were being pulled up from the past, that were fueling our future,
Our ancestors made mistakes that we never learnt from,
And what we have to endure now will never be worth it,
People say that it isn't our forefathers' fault,
But we all know deep down that it is.

Our lives had never been so deprived of privacy, nor our lands so divided,
We had all been brought up with disillusion and rivalry, yet none of that prepared us for what we had to face,
The attacks are relentless,
Our hope is deserting us,
The peace never lasts long enough.
The sky burns an endless fiery red,

However, in the midst of it all, something always seems to keep us going,
Through the famine, hostilities and downfalls,
And I hope because of this, one day there will be peace.

## Ava Robinson (12)
Cottingham High School, Cottingham

# Friendship

Friendship is a joy,
It's a prized gem,
A diamond in the rough.
But how do you know where to look?
Where to dig?
It's a gamble,
But it's worth it.

An argument with a friend can be playful,
Nothing important.
But it can be intense and wounding.
Even just a tiny disagreement,
Could end in heartache.
It can be mended,
But only if you have the willpower,
And others to support you.
How do you know what will be the last thing you say to a friend?
What if you can never take back a bad mistake?
Will it ever be the same again?
What move is the right one to make?
Is it worth the risk of losing someone?

A heart is fragile,
Like glass, it's easy to break.
Some hearts are frozen and chained,
Hiding away from any love or affection.

Others are open to anything,
Love and hate, broken much more easily,
But they aways bounce back,
No matter how long it takes them.
That's life.

Friendship makes life complete,
Whether it be one friend or more.
Everyone needs at least one,
Or how else do you carry on?

**Iyesha Wilson (13)**
Cottingham High School, Cottingham

# What Do You See?

What do you see?
A juicy steak?
A joint of roast beef? Or
An eccentric cow stuck in a pen,
With hardly any room?
Stuck in a pen,
Taken away from its mother,
At just a few minutes old,
Being force-fed til fat,
Killed brutally,
To be on your plate.

What do you see? A leg of lamb?
A chunk of mutton? Or
A jolly little lamb stuck in a pen?
Just months old, then
*Bang!*
A dead little creature in the middle of a room,
To be on your plate.

What do you see?
A chicken breast?
A tender drumstick? Or
A fluffy little bird stuck in a barn?
Removed from mother,
Force-fed too much,
Unable to stand,

Feathers removed,
To be on your plate.

To be on your plate
These animals go through horrible experiences,
And yet consumers dismiss
What has happened and
Don't show gratefulness for this 'food',
And refuse to accept that the cruel
Treatment these animals go through
To be on your plate.

What do you see?
A piece of meat?
Or a stolen life?

## Eliza Mann-Berue (12)
Cottingham High School, Cottingham

# The Darkness He Loves

In the depths of her soul,
An ancient church stands.
Weathered stones, silent prayers,
Held by unseen hands.
Her presence, a sanctuary,
Serene and profound.
In her quiet grace and beauty,
Mysteries abound.

Like stained-glass windows, her eyes reveal,
Stories untold, emotions concealed.
In the shadowed aisles of her heart's embrace,
Love finds solace, adorned yet with no trace.

Yet she is also the crow, dark and wise,
With secrets whispered, beneath midnight skies.
Her laughter, a melody of twilight's call,
In her flight, shadows dance and darkness falls.

Love with her is a journey through the night,
Where stars illuminate the depths of sight.
In her darkness, he finds the light,
In her silence, he hears the flight.

Through storms and shadows, they find their light,
Together they soar, like crows in flight.
In her ancient church of emotions, where her feelings lay,
Love finds its way.

And in her darkness,
He chooses to stay.

## Samuel Hodgson (13)
Cottingham High School, Cottingham

# Death Row Is Waiting

Sentenced to death,
A life behind bars,

*Tick-tock.*

Long, lonely hours,
Waiting for my fate,

*Tick-tock.*

Right to be punished,
Extinguishing a life,

*Tick-tock.*

Going to meet my maker,
My final judgement day,

*Tick-tock.*

The waiting is the hardest,
Not knowing when it will be,

*Tick-tock.*

My appeal is unsuccessful,
The end is now near,

*Tick-tock.*

Choosing my final meal,
My last taste of life,

*Tick-tock.*

Heart racing wildly,
They've arrived at my cell,

*Tick-tock.*

Legs like jelly,
Every step a second less to live,

*Tick-tock.*

I kneel down,
Excelling towards my doom,

*Tick-tock.*

My time is over,
As I take my final breath,

Chop chop,

Silence...

## Noah Watkins (12)
Cottingham High School, Cottingham

# On The Edge Of Despair: A Suicidal Shadow

In shadows deep where light does fade,
I dwell alone in endless shade.
With a heavy heart and burdened soul,
I wonder lost without control.

The world around, a blurry haze,
each passing moment just a daze.
In silent screams my spirit cries,
as hope dissolves and darkness lies.

The weight of life is too much to bear,
I long to flee, to anywhere.
To escape the pain that grips my mind,
and leave this evil world behind.

Yet in the depths, the darkness calls,
a tempting void where sorrow falls.
I teeter on the edge unsure
of what my shattered heart endures.

So here I stand upon the brink,
a fragile soul too scared to sink.
But in my darkness I find release,
for even in despair there is no peace.

With a heavy heart and weary eyes,
I bid farewell to endless skies.
Silent sorrow I resign,
to let the darkness make me mine.

### Jessica Danyi (13)
Cottingham High School, Cottingham

# Glue

I'm tired,
I'm tired of my family.
I'm tired,
I'm tired of school.
I'm tired,
I'm tired of the arguments.
I'm tired,
I'm tired of being responsible.
I don't want to be,
The glue of my friends
Family,
I'm tired.
But by being the glue,
I keep my parents happy,
I stick them together.
I keep my friends happy,
I stick them back together.
As long as my loved ones are happy,
I am.
I can stick the smiles on them,
Maybe being responsible for happiness,
Is okay.

### Will Grady (13)
Cottingham High School, Cottingham

# Every Day Is The Same

Every day, I do what I'm told,
Like an alarm clock at the crack of dawn,
Waiting to be shut off,
I have freedom? Sure,
But would one really call being bombarded with the press,
At my gates,
Or the stress that I absolutely hate,
With a burning passion,
Freedom? What if I don't want to dress,
In all this fancy fashion,
Or follow this strict code?
All I want to do is turn old,
In the comfort of my abode,
None of this matters,
Because very soon,
I will inevitably pop,
Just like a balloon.

**Jack Butler (13)**
Cottingham High School, Cottingham

# Teen Drama

**T** eenage life is complicated and tragic,
**E** veryone is staring 'cause I look like messed-up magic,
**E** arly life should not be hard,
**N** either should teenage girls be harmed.

**D** raining work throughout the day,
**R** uthless students will stop to say,
**A** nyone could do better than you!
**M** any other girls believe it is true,
**A** lways remember, you are braver than you believe, stronger than you seem, smarter than you seem and twice as beautiful as you'd ever imagine.

## Alice Dobbs (12)
Cottingham High School, Cottingham

# Journeys Of Hope

Their lives are ruined,
Their lives are gone,
They are refugees.

Guns hammering,
Glass shattering,
They are refugees.

Borders crossed in fear,
Holding loved ones near,
They are refugees.

Dreams left behind,
Yet hope they still find,
They are refugees.

Their tales untold,
Of walking through the cold,
They are refugees.

The world must help the ones in need,
They are the refugees.

**Louisa Shepherdson (13)**
Cottingham High School, Cottingham

# Criminal Cat

I sat on a bin and looked around,
Until suddenly, I heard a sound.
I was curious so I peered below,
What it was, I had to know.
Suddenly a man appeared,
He had bright white hair and a long white beard.
The man pulled out a gun,
He didn't look fun.
"Give me the money,
Or you won't find this funny."
My owner hit him with a pan,
And then we both ran.
We heard sirens behind us,
But they would never find us.

## Max Wilson (12)
Cottingham High School, Cottingham

# I Used To Live

I used to live on the great, green sea stack,
I used to live on a coral reef,
I used to live in the great forest of kelp.

The people made it a short thing,
With a tall tower,
Leading oil-belching metal wave cutters away.

The people made it a white, rubble ghost town,
With an oil-sucking machine on top.

The people made it,
A barren stretch of sand,
Perfect for their fish-napping, fish-trapping objects.

**Matilda Keane (12)**
Cottingham High School, Cottingham

# The Soldier

I am on a mission.
I am here to fight.
I am here to serve.
I am with an army.

I am on a mission.
My heart is beating.
My legs are burning.
My goal is simple.

I am on a mission.
To defend the weak.
To save their lives.
To take them home.

I am on a mission.
I am breaking in.
I am falling down.
I have made my sacrifice.

I was on a mission.
I am a soldier.

## James Nalson (11)
Cottingham High School, Cottingham

# Changing World

**E** very piece of rubbish,
**N** obody cares.
**V** ital but not looked after.
**I** n secret water rises,
**R** aging storms and droughts,
**O** ver and over again.
**N** o food or clean water,
**M** ankind doesn't think.
**E** ver changing world,
**N** o one realises nature is dying,
**T** ime is ticking until it's too late.

## Mason Edmond (11)
Cottingham High School, Cottingham

# Every Night

As I listen to the child,
Raging and ranting,
All I can do
Is embrace him.

He rages,
Worries,
And all I do
Is stand there.

I listen to his worries,
And listen to his panic.
All I am able to do
Is watch him.

When he finishes,
He falls asleep, panicked for the next day.
All I can do,
Is hold him.

## Zak Robinson (14)
Cottingham High School, Cottingham

# The Fear Of The Spear!

In my eye,
Slaughter,
Slain,
Stalking,
It's a game of cat and mouse.

Capture,
Caught,
Culling,
I hear the poacher shout.

Attack,
Ambush,
Assault,
In pain all day and night.

Snare,
Seek,
Shoot,
It's time to charge, take flight.

## Frances Young (13)
Cottingham High School, Cottingham

# A Teen Life

As I walk down the hall
These girls I hate call
"Shorty!"
"Pity
Nobody likes a fatty"
Like, I've been drained all day,
I don't need this today.
Finally as I exit,
Every day when I arrive, I want to leg it.

## Lily Cook (12)
Cottingham High School, Cottingham

## Sweet Baby James

*A haiku*

James likes dinosaurs,
He knows all their names by heart,
He is only two.

### Robert Roper (12)
Cottingham High School, Cottingham

# The War Photographer Man

Armed with a camera,
Scattered across the front line,
A man took some photos,
Hobbling in his stride.

The pictures showed a story,
Of tales lost long ago,
Stories of pain and glory,
Ones of tragedy, ones of love.

The photos were plastered everywhere,
The billboards and signposts,
But the people walked right past them,
And the photographer became a ghost.

He sat alone in his dollhouse,
In shattered pieces of glass,
As he relived the war, all over,
Faces come alive in the dark.

## Freya Davies (15)
Eltham Hill School, Eltham Hill

# True Me

Staring in the mirror, analysing my appearance
My long, flowing hair and feminine features
But my heart refuses to let that be me
My boyish clothes – baggy T-shirt and jeans
Scissors inch towards my hair
But my mind cries that nobody will accept me
Heart or mind, I struggle to choose
Boy or girl, I struggle to choose
I act so girly, yet I am so boyish
Both choices are full of pros and cons
What will everyone say?
Would it be seen as a betrayal to be me?
No longer their little girl
They'd be so disappointed
One more feeling speaks out to me...
"Be you," it shouts. "Trust me!"
But how can you follow yourself
If you're struggling to choose what defines yourself?
Lowering the scissors, letting out a sigh
I distance myself from the mirror
Ignoring my heart, mind and gut feeling
Knowing this feeling will loop round and round again...

## Harley Johnstone (12)
Fleetwood High School, Fleetwood

# Twisted Fantasy

The pain you caused me,
You can't see through your twisted fantasy.
My pain you don't see,
Yet it is shown so clearly.

The trauma we went through,
Everyone has said it to you,
The trauma you gave me, like a soldier at war,
When you reach out to me you wonder why I close the door.

A mother you claim to be,
But you never raised me.
I raised myself,
Because every time I asked, I would receive a pelt,
He'd beat us with his belt.
Yet you comfort him, you traitor,
Saying it's human nature.

Lie after lie,
Only caring about us when we're about to die,
The pain you caused,
You seem to forget,
Living in your twisted fantasy,
Without any regret.

Even after these fifteen excruciating years,
And all of these silent, unheard tears,

I bear all the weight of the problems -
Still raising your children.

You ignore my warnings and pleas,
Saying Dad is hurting us,
But you comfort him, you traitor,
Saying it's just human nature,
And yet you yearn for this shattered trust,
Knowing full well the trauma you inflicted upon us makes it bust.

I saw problems before they arose; before they could cause trouble,
Yet you refuse to leave your paradise, your bubble.
That mental fantasy where you hide away,
To escape reality where you physically obey,
That man who claims he loves you,
But I know the truth,
The dark secrets that take light,
I show you them but you look through them like they're not in sight.

I called for you each time he kicked, punched or harmed us,
Your response was, "Stop being childish and grow up."
Now even after he's gone,
You show off this dysfunctional family
Like it's some sort of trophy.
Even after these fifteen excruciating years,
And after all these silent, unheard tears,

You're still the same,
You only need me when it's something you gain.

## Lily Hesketh (15)
Fleetwood High School, Fleetwood

# Relationships

Jeremy Ray Taylor is one of my close friends
Finn WolfhArd is my best friend
Chosen Jacobs the guy that plays Mike Hanlon
Eddie Kaspbrak is my role in it

Finn WolfharD is my best friend that I met in the cast
Yungk2x is my TikTok account
Losers Club is Eddie's group
Asher Angel is my second-best buddy
CalpurNia is Finn's music band

Giulia is my friend in Luca
Finn WolfhaRd, famous for Stranger Things
Asher Angel is the main kid in Shazam
Zachary Levi, met him on Shazam cast
AshEr Angel, also met on Shazam cast
Jeremy Ray Taylor is Sunny in Goosebumps 2.

## Gracie Leddy (11)
Fleetwood High School, Fleetwood

# The Greatest Game In History For Darwin Núñez

Stepping onto the pitch gives me shivers
Wanting to come out as winners
Hearing the crowd cheering as loud as an aeroplane
The weight on my shoulders, as heavy as weights
With the title on the line, we need to win
Shaking hands with our opponents
Staring at the crowd with pride
Not wanting to let them down
The whistle blows
Everything goes silent
Szoboszlai takes the centre kick and passes it to Virgil
He sends the ball long to Luis Díaz
He wins the header
"Amazing Lucho," I shout (Luis in Colombian)
The ball slowly slides into the corner flag
Mac Allister collects the ball and rainbow flicks the defender
He crosses the ball with pace into the penalty area
I see the ball, just behind me, I know what to do
I hear the commentator shout, "Darwin Núñez!"
I go for the bicycle kick and score!
"Best goal in the history of the Champions League!"
Everything in the newspaper is about my goal
What a game I'm having
In the 37th minute, I scored again, this time from the halfway line

"Man of the Match," the commentator said
2-0 up at half-time in the Champions League final
Klopp said to me, "I knew you could do it."
Playing with confidence and then in the 79th minute
I scored a brace, 3-0
The scenes are insane
The final whistle goes
I collapse to my knees crying with joy
"Darwin, Darwin Núñez he came from Benfica to big reds," the crowd chant again and again
We won
I can't believe it
My hat-trick won us the Champions League trophy
3-0 against Real Madrid at full time
Walking off the pitch with the weight off my shoulders
And a match ball
We lift the trophy
My dream came true
Everyone is talking about how I'm the best and how well I played
Everyone loves me!

## Thomas Cameron (12)
Fleetwood High School, Fleetwood

# I Still Love You

You betrayed me,
Be happy, but not as happy as you were with me,
As I drove to your house,
As quiet as a mouse,
You left the door open,
Hoping you would see me,
But you're too busy staring into her eyes,
I despise you,
All I wanted was love that lasts,
With you forever,
But now you're gone,
Don't tell me you're sorry,
But feel sorry for yourself,
I tried to be tough,
I tried to be mean,
Even after all, I still love you,
Sometimes I try to understand,
Why you would do this all to me,
Are you insecure? Unhappy?
But I loved you truly,
Just laugh at the stupidity,
But I was the one who showed you the place,
Also told you about Billy Joel,
You're sharing it with her now,
But please don't forget me,
And that I still love you...

**Hallie Butler (12)**
Fleetwood High School, Fleetwood

# Natascha Kampusch's Story

Natascha Kampusch, a tale of strength untold
My life of resilience
My story to behold.
I was kidnapped at a tender age,
My world turned dark,
But within me a spark, a fire, a remarkable mark.

For years in captivity, I endured
My spirit unbroken, my will secured.
Through walls of isolation, I found my way
Holding onto hope, day after day.
In the depths of despair, I never lost sight,
Dreaming of freedom, yearning for light.

With courage as my guide
I made my escape
Breaking the chains that held me
No longer a captive
Natascha, a symbol of resilience and grace
A survivor who triumphed, finding my place.

My story reminds me of the strength I possess
To overcome adversity, to rise and progress.

## Eleanor Cox (12)
Fleetwood High School, Fleetwood

# Friends

I can see my friends up there,
Gliding up so high.
With the wind beneath their wings,
They dance through the sky.

I can see my friends up there,
Twirling in the light.
Their beautiful fresh feathers,
Shining in the night.

I can see my friends up there,
Their lives just begun.
But I'll never leave the nest,
Till my life is done.

I can see my friends up there,
But they can't see me.
I'm the failure of the clutch,
To never be set free.

My friends come to my nest,
Only passing by.
And my final chance to give them,
A fleeting last goodbye.

I can't see my friends up there,
But I will never fly.
I'm just left to wait and wait,
Till the day I die.

## Lily Holden (15)
Fleetwood High School, Fleetwood

# The Match

Walking on the pitch, all my problems disappeared,
The referee blew his whistle,
It started...
Fans cheering for their team,
Suddenly, the other team came attacking to me,
I stood in my net, ready for the shot,
It went past me,
Ssh!
The referee's whistle blew for half-time,
Hungry for the team to win, we carried on,
My team began to run towards the goal,
The striker was one on one with the keeper and scored to make it 1-1,
It was close to the end of the match now,
In the last minute, we won a corner,
Knowing what I had to do, I went up the pitch for the corner,
The ball floated into the box, I jumped up and headed it into the back of the net,
The crowd was screaming my name,
I did it.

**Alex Pook (12)**
Fleetwood High School, Fleetwood

# I Am Bukayo Saka

He is darting down the right wing once again,
But four years ago he lost the final.
It was the Euro final against Italy
It went to penalties
Saka stepped up, he shot. *Oooh!*
He just missed.
All you could hear was the Italian crowd cheering.
Italy were the European Champions.

It was the next day.
I took a look on Twitter and saw someone had posted something...
That fan was banned from going to football matches.
I took a few matches off.
It is now 2024
And I am one of the best wingers in the Premier League.
I just scored a match-winner
I do my signature celebration in front of the Arsenal fans
Arsenal are on top.
I am Bukayo Saka.

## Christopher Pochin (11)
Fleetwood High School, Fleetwood

# The Policeman

I got shot by a policeman.
Because of my skin colour.
The policeman said that I had a gun.
But the policeman didn't look in my pockets.
The policeman just shot me
And I was only a young boy.
I didn't do anything.
I don't understand.
The last thing I heard was my ma
Crying in the background.
I'm a ghost now
And my ma has been sleeping in my bed at night.
Grandma has been watching me
Standing near the TV.
She looked my way when I followed Ma into the living room.
I think my grandma can sense me.
The funeral is coming up in a few days.
Ma wants my coffin open so everyone can see
What the policeman has done to me.

## Lacie Atkin (11)
Fleetwood High School, Fleetwood

# Teenage Dreams

My dream is to be the most popular person in the school,
But we all know that won't happen,
I have spots on my face,
I wear glasses and I have bright red hair,
The girls at school hate me,
They place chewing gum in my hair,
I did nothing wrong,
But I guess if you're ugly,
No one will love you,
Even though no one seemed to love me,
There was one person who talked to me every day,
Sat with me at lunch,
And told me I was pretty,
She stood up for me when I was being bullied,
And told me I was her best friend,
Don't bully, be kind, treat people how you want to be treated,
And remember,
Everyone is pretty in their own way.

## Louisa Beech (11)
Fleetwood High School, Fleetwood

# Holiday

I step out of the plane, the smile on my face,
I'm going to have a fun time getting used to this place,
I arrive at my hotel, I'm in my room,
I step out on the balcony and see the bright moon,
I walk to the beach all alone,
Nothing but me and my phone,
I hear my ringtone,
It's my mum calling me home,
I leap into my bed, hoping for a good rest,
I think about tomorrow, it's going to be the best,
My holiday is nearly up now,
I dearly love this place,
I wish I could stay here forever, but that's not the case,
I pack my suitcase ready for the flight,
I make sure to prepare everything for the night.

**Jake Warburton (12)**
Fleetwood High School, Fleetwood

# Trustworthy

I am starting high school, too nervous to go in
A big group of girls walks past with large, sinister grins
The teacher takes me inside
The school is strong and sturdy, but I think it's a house of lies
The bell finally rings. It's time to go on our break
I whisper under my breath, "Make some friends, for goodness' sake"
I step up to someone, waving my hand hi
She just looks at me and rolls her eyes
I sit in the corner, starting to cry
Some girl walks up to me and says, "Are you alright?"
And that is the end of my demise.

## Belle Martin (11)
Fleetwood High School, Fleetwood

# The Death Of A Prisoner

Just sitting here in this chair,
Thinking when I would be here,
It's been a month since my arrest,
So brutal and tense,
Two police officers are guarding my stall,
One so little and one so tall,
I don't want to be here anymore,
I've been trapped here for a month,
I just want to be let free,
So I can be a good teen,
Why does the year have to go slow?
The guard is looking at me straight in the eye,
Asking who am I?
I don't know what will happen to me now,
Will I bring myself down?

**Lexi-Leigh MacDonald (12)**
Fleetwood High School, Fleetwood

# The Last Judgement

I reach the court, I am deemed guilty,
My family watch as tears stream down their face,
And I realise that the chair will be my fate.
I am handed my last meal,
But I can tell it's the real deal,
I am seated down on the chair,
Yet all I get is one last glare.
My world is filled with shades of grey,
I know today will be my last day.
I follow through the tunnel to the light,
Not much longer, and it won't be bright.
I regret all the choices that I have made,
Suddenly, the light begins to fade.

## Daniel Dadson (12)
Fleetwood High School, Fleetwood

## Positive Thoughts

**N** ever give up.
**E** ighty-two was the age I died
**I** n the United Air Force
**L** anding on the moon was fun, I think.

**A** ugust 5th 1930 was when I was born
**R** ocket science is fun to me
**M** usical talents I would like to think
**S** tay strong even in bad times if you can
**T** ill I was sixteen I had my pilot's licence
**R** esilience is key, I'd want to believe
**O** hio is my hometown
**N** ASA is where I worked
**G** ive it your all.

**Lilly-Mai Walker (12)**
Fleetwood High School, Fleetwood

# The Equaliser

It was the second half,
And we were two-nil down.
I ran with the ball.
Passed it to my teammate,
He scored!
It was now two-one.
It was the ninety-sixth minute now.
My teammate got a free kick.
He wanted to take it.
I picked up the ball and placed it down.
I took my run-up,
And it went in the top corner!
I was running up to the corner flag, celebrating.
All my teammates were running up to me.
The ref blew the whistle.
But we were worried,
It was time for pens...

## Nadia Salthouse (12)
Fleetwood High School, Fleetwood

# Watchers

Running through an alleyway,
Never touching the people who stare,
Black figures everywhere,
*Don't speak, the watchers don't like it*
Echoes through my head,
 **W** atching people everywhere,
 **A** nywhere I go,
 **T** oo many people,
 **C** aught in a web of shadowy figures,
 **H** idden in the shadows, they stand,
 **E** very minute of my life, they're everywhere,
 **R** eally scary people are with me twenty-four seven,
 **S** hadowy people.

## Simon Shaw (12)
Fleetwood High School, Fleetwood

# Wasting Away

Wasting away,
Skin and bones,
Recovery or death.

The scales mock me,
The mirror is two-faced,
They can't show or quantify how I feel inside.

I look in the mirror,
A person I do not like stares back at me,
Big, ugly, unwanted, unloved,
Are words that come to mind when I look at me.

The scales mock me,
The mirror is two-faced,
They can't show or quantify how I feel inside.

Wasting away,
Skin and bones,
Recovery or death.

**Star Elliott (11)**
Fleetwood High School, Fleetwood

# Untitled

Imprisoned in the attic.
One pen, one book.
Over and over, every day.
Looking through the circular window.
Writing everything I see.
Family stressing, sister sobbing.
When will it end?
Staying quiet, not wanting to be found.
If it goes wrong I'm going down.
Too scared to leave, too scared to breathe.
Not eating to save food.
It has been a couple of weeks and I'm starting to get drained.
Too tired to walk, too tired to talk.
When will it end?

**Pixie-lee Tavernor (11)**
Fleetwood High School, Fleetwood

# Pineapple On Pizza

People hate me
I don't even know why
Not many people will try me
Enough is enough
Always picked off
Pepperoni hates me too
Places don't even advertise me
Ignored or scrolled past all the time
Excuses, 'I'm allergic', you just don't like me
Or having me removed
Never me, I'm always last
Please try me
I'm not just a fruit, I'm a topping too
Zucchini is one though
Zucchini is a fruit as well
All alone.

## Lexi Rees (12)
Fleetwood High School, Fleetwood

# A Circus Cheetah

I remember being in the wild night,
Hunting was the biggest highlight,
Chasing my prey,
Now I am being chased on display,
The bright lights dance in front of my eyes,
I miss the fresh air and the stars in the deep blue skies,
I used to be as happy as a bunny,
Now everybody laughs and says I am funny,
I'm a predator, you would all fear me,
If it wasn't for these bars containing me with a key,
Get me out, get me out,
I miss being able to run about.

**Tiffany Tseneva (12)**
Fleetwood High School, Fleetwood

# Prisoner Life

Oh, prison, why are you so big?
So we cannot get out,
Prison is the best,
We are alone,
Free but not too free so that we will get out,
But why, oh, why do we have to go to prison when we are bad?
All we did was a crime,
But it can be fun being naughty,
We have lots of fun,
But some of us did nothing,
I feel bad for the people who did nothing,
Prison is a thing that we go to if we are bad,
The police may be able to stop us,
But not anyone else.

## Samuel Newton (12)
Fleetwood High School, Fleetwood

# Marcus Rashford

Losing, missing penalties,
Rubbish free kicks, putting up with hate comments,
Getting injured, starting on the bench,
Not playing a full game, listening to racist comments.

The other half,
Never giving up, being positive,
Scoring free kicks, putting up with hate comments,
Scoring penalties, winning games,
Getting into the final, winning cup games.

Leads to one day playing for England,
Scoring a last-minute goal to win the World Cup.

## Lexi Myerscough (11)
Fleetwood High School, Fleetwood

## Social Media

Hiding behind the screen,
Scrolling, scrolling,
Not knowing what to expect,
Bullying, laughing,
Every day the same thing,
Over and over,
Texting and crying,
Wanting to end it,
Staring at the screen,
Wanting to see what happens,
No one to trust,
No one to speak to,
A little girl, broken inside,
Alone,
Where do I go?
Too scared to scream,
Too scared to holler,
Walking to school with sweat around my collar.

### Isabelle Lloyd (12)
Fleetwood High School, Fleetwood

# Pretend Friends

I wasn't like them,
But I could pretend,
We shone like a gem,
I knew it would end,
I loved them until lunar,
I was such a fool,
Played like an untuned guitar,
I drowned in their thorn-filled pool,
Before I knew,
They became my bully,
Time suddenly flew,
I still couldn't process fully,
Soon this would stop like a call,
It would all come to an end,
Because, after all,
They were just my pretend friend.

**Evelyn Clough (11)**
Fleetwood High School, Fleetwood

# Anne Frank

Anne Frank was a scared girl
Who lived in a dark world
It was constant war, war
She wanted to walk out the door, door
She couldn't help but say, "No, no"
This world was a no-go
She was dragged from home to a camp
It was like a battle ramp
She got killed in a gas chamber
Only her dad survived. He was a lifesaver
He got her diary, completed it and sent it
Off to the church, so they could help him a lot.

## Skye Taylor (12)
Fleetwood High School, Fleetwood

# Blood, Blood And More Blood

Blood and gore,
Every day more and more,
Bombs fly,
Soaring sky-high,
People are dying,
Presidents are lying.

Take cover,
Go to your mother,
Businesses are ruined,
What are you doing?
Death is what I see,
Please, someone, come save me.

Soldiers firing guns,
Bakers offering cream buns,
Trying to make everyone feel better,
While I write this letter,
Russia, please let us be.

**Daisy Kelly-Rutherford (12)**
Fleetwood High School, Fleetwood

# Anne Frank

I took my freedom for granted, but now I'm trapped.
I am now all alone while the world is in pieces.
My family and I are starving.
The rest of us ran, but they got taken.
We are running.
We are being shoved into the back of an army truck.
They are taking us to a concentration camp.
I have a feeling I don't have long left.
We are being loaded into a gas chamber.
My family are screaming.
We are all dead.

## Amelia Calligan (11)
Fleetwood High School, Fleetwood

# Under The Box...

The aroma filled the room as the Domino's pizza was dropped off
It was dark at first, then the grease-covered box widened
People surrounded me, then left me stranded
My fruity pineapple taste was never a base
I had a creamy doughy start
Which I thought was a fart!
Tomato-based puree was covered like lipstick stains
Then I realised I was to blame
"Pineapple or none," they say
I wish I never stayed.

## Megan Morrissey (12)
Fleetwood High School, Fleetwood

# The Pizza With Pineapple

I'm just another pizza,
Another ordinary pizza.
With dreams to one day become a chosen pizza,
Or maybe even an eaten pizza.
Here I lie on the pizza tray,
Topped with all the same ingredients the others have.
Except I have pineapple on top of me,
Pineapple pizza! What a disgrace!
Abandoned and hated by all pizza lovers,
I'm just another pizza.
Another ordinary pizza,
Try not to judge without trying a pizza.

## Mollie Wood (12)
Fleetwood High School, Fleetwood

# The Life And Death Of A Soldier

I live to die,
Fight to live,
But I only shoot to see the smiles of my family,
The cheers of my peers,
I know we've won,
I'm coming home,
My family's over the moon,
We celebrate for hours,
Then I'm shipped off again,
*Bang* is *beeps*,
The cries of my family,
The *beep* fades thin,
A figure says, "At ease, soldier,"
Now I know I'm gone.

## Yoshi Robson (12)
Fleetwood High School, Fleetwood

# Hate Letter To Alcohol

You're the reason I got my a** kicked,
I wish there was another option I could have picked,
But you're the only way to drown my silence,
I wish there was a way out of violence,
A chrome wiring thrown in from the side,
I'd thought I'd die,
I sit there all night and I cry,
I had thirty-two teeth in my mouth,
But some went away,
My pockets were empty from all the drinks I had to pay.

**Alfie Morgan (12)**
Fleetwood High School, Fleetwood

# Not My Fault

I could feel myself getting red,
All these voices in my head,
What happened?
It was so fast,
As my car left last,
I wonder what he's doing now,
While I suffer and drown,
As I rot in this hell,
Nothing is changing in this cell,
Another call, what's it now?
Oh god, a laundry job,
Please not me, I will sob,
I could feel myself getting red,
All these voices in my head.

### Katie Balmer (12)
Fleetwood High School, Fleetwood

# Mr Beast's Thoughts Of Economy

**M** any companies are hungry for money

**R** eckless, stopping at nothing to release new products

**B** easts risen from hell, leaving others in shadows

**E** conomy is equal to corruption, takes control of everyone

**A** ll the CEOs sit in luxury while others starve

**S** afety isn't a problem when you have bodyguards with you

**T** rust is a mind game when economy is involved.

## Jaidan Lyall (12)
Fleetwood High School, Fleetwood

# They Tell Me I Can Fly, But All I Do Is Cry

My parents tell me to just try,
but all I feel I can do is cry and ask why.
Some friends will come and go, just like how the wind can blow.
They tell me I cry like a girl and I should grow up, but when I try to grow up,
I feel I have to shut up even if I need to throw up.
My family say I'm rude,
but they don't understand how I feel blue,
I have to hold my tears, I might as well disappear.

**Layla Fuller (12)**
Fleetwood High School, Fleetwood

# Hostage

The sun is setting, the stars come out,
I'm locked in a box, trying to scream and shout,
There are people surrounding me,
I think one of them is a she,
I'm on my knees, crying,
I don't know what to do,
There's no escape,
My mouth is taped,
I'm held hostage,
I really need help,
I'm in an abandoned place,
They've taken everything,
Have mercy!

### Alfie Brown (11)
Fleetwood High School, Fleetwood

# Being A Teen

Being a teen
It's hard sometimes
All the bullying, shouting and racism too
*Boo hoo*
It's good but not great
It can be fun
All the friends
Some stay, some go
Social media too
But be careful
There are creeps about
Trying to date
But as long as I keep my personal information to myself
I will be okay
But besides that
Being a teen is great!

## Lily Willacy-Dodd (11)
Fleetwood High School, Fleetwood

# Goalkeeper

The ball swerved from left to right
It flew over me, what a fright,
The sound of the crowd as they shout my name,
I think this could be my last game.

The world was watching
All eyes on me as I fell down on my knees,
My head hurts, the pain fills my head,
I bet most people want me dead.

What was I doing?
My career is done,
The legend I once was,
Is now gone.

## Kyle Dewett (12)
Fleetwood High School, Fleetwood

# I Am

There I am
Gliding through the streets
Everybody staring at me
Thinking to myself
I am only an ordinary plastic bag
Roaming around the streets
Is it because I am green?
Is it because I am rubbish?
Lots of new places to see
So many cars
So many roads
It is like a whole new planet
That I have never been to
And still
No one has picked me up.

**Poppy Howell (11)**
Fleetwood High School, Fleetwood

# War

It's been an hour since I was brought here,
Time flies by when you stare at the stormy sky,
*Bang!*
Gunshots echo and deafen me inside,
I walk through the deep mud as innocent people scream,
I run until I can't anymore,
More bullets fly past me but I continue,
This is war, a world war,
Don't beg for it to happen,
Because war is here.

## Alfie Stanley (12)
Fleetwood High School, Fleetwood

# The Blood Drips

Distant screeching travels the air,
What's going on?
Everything is a blur.
I'm dizzy.
Why did I do that?
Questions swirl through my head.
I am aching, itching, *burning!*
Where is everyone?
*Brrrrrrrrrrr!* rings around the room.
Gunshots chime in my head.
Don't black lives matter?
Well, I guess not.

**Lillie Hatcher (12)**
Fleetwood High School, Fleetwood

# Where Are You?

Screaming and crying,
I feel like I'm dying,
I'm drinking away
At a bottle of Chardonnay,
Taking my pills to stop the pain,
I don't think I'm sane,
Grasping onto the memory of you,
While the posters are flying in my view,
I've drunk too much
While you've been out of my clutch,
Where are you?

**Pippa Wilson (12)**
Fleetwood High School, Fleetwood

# Sally's New Phone

It was Sally's birthday,
Hip-hip-hooray,
Sally got a phone,
As she yelped in a thankful tone,
But as the day went on,
Her life seemed gone.

Sally was addicted,
But at the table, she spilt some liquid,
Her phone wouldn't turn on,
Sally was horrified,
"Oh no," she moaned.

**Sonny Prior (11)**
Fleetwood High School, Fleetwood

# Messi

Lionel Messi is the GOAT,
Sitting in his ten-million-dollar boat.
But he doesn't like to gloat,
Even though he's sailing on his ten-million-dollar boat.
He has a load of watches,
Fame, clothes and multiple brands.
He scores more goals than Ronaldo,
When Messi scores, they all go, "Woah!"

**Oscar Dudley (11)**
Fleetwood High School, Fleetwood

# Prisoner Of The Brain

As I lie in my tomb
The ceiling goes *boom!*
And the rats scurry out of the door.
"I'm imagining," I say, "this is all a dream.
I want to see my family."
I need to escape from this nightmare
Where artillery rings, guns fire and bombs fall
As soldiers walk past the cell.

## Ryan Jennison (11)
Fleetwood High School, Fleetwood

# Death Row Awaiting

D eath is awaiting.
E very second makes me angrier
A nd every minute ticks down.
T he last meal is cooking.
H eavy sweat is falling down my cuffs like rain.

R age is pouring into me.
O n the death bed I lie
W aiting for the growing pain to stop.

## Jack Roberts (11)
Fleetwood High School, Fleetwood

# Being A Dog

Being a dog is kinda fun
I get a treat for doing tricks
Toys to play with
Cuddles too
But being a dog can be tough
Not being able to say when you need the loo
Getting shouted at when chewing on a shoe
But barking at squirrels and chasing balls can be tiring
So cuddles with my owners are nice.

## Lilly-Jayne Morton (12)
Fleetwood High School, Fleetwood

# Beavo's Story

I'm Beavo
I get bullied because my teeth are lopsided
Everyone calls me a beaver
And I can't chew either
So it's hard for me to eat
But I started a social media account
My famous quote is "Big up."
I've been getting a lot of support from my community,
So... big up.

## Tyler Pendlebury (11)
Fleetwood High School, Fleetwood

## 13 Unlucky Lines

I've been evicted,
I feel restricted,
I'm all alone,
I feel lost.
I see a war,
I think it's against the law,
As I start to pack my bag,
My brain begins to lag,
As I throw away my key,
A tear runs down my cheek,
I wish I were safe,
Who am I?
I am a refugee.

**Peter Smith (11)**
Fleetwood High School, Fleetwood

# That One Night

**S** creaming in pain,
**C** ircular wheel, ground up the ramp,
**O** ver my head, the scooter goes,
**O** n the floor, I go,
**T** he bars stabbed my liver,
**E** R trip, again I shall go,
**R** ound two, I shall do,
**S** creaming in happiness, because I finally landed it.

## Troy Stott (12)
Fleetwood High School, Fleetwood

# Charity

I was at the mall,
I saw a kid crying against the wall,
His parents seemed to not be there,
I gave him a ball and then escorted him down the hall
Where his parents were.
After that, I gave all the kids in Africa 100 pears,
They were all very thankful,
There was one named Frank who was full!

**Alexander Hill (12)**
Fleetwood High School, Fleetwood

# Family Counts

**F** riends to everyone that can care.
**A** nimals to people but never speak.
**M** akes everyone happy to live their life.
**I** ll or not, family cares.
**L** ove surrounding everyone always there.
**Y** ours and mine, we love them all, let's get together and have a ball.

## Alexus Kennedy (11)
Fleetwood High School, Fleetwood

# The Young Boy Called Marcus

In my childhood, I was poor,
Then, I became something more.
The rain, cascading, hit the ground,
My dog was spinning round and round.

I tried to join a football team,
Wearing colours matching the theme.
Finally, here, my dream came true,
Then, I was a part of their crew.

## Tiarna Quinn (12)
Fleetwood High School, Fleetwood

## Everything Has Changed

**C** overed in robots
**H** eaps of litter everywhere
**A** l that covers the internet
**N** o jobs available
**G** uns being used too much
**E** verybody always on their phones
**D** eath rates getting higher.

This is not right.

### Lucy Rayworth (12)
Fleetwood High School, Fleetwood

## My Life As A YouTuber

**M** y life as a YouTuber is exciting and fun,
**R** ich,

**B** east burger,
**E** ating feastable bars,
**A** lmost got cancelled, I feel sad,
**S** aving people makes me feel good,
**T** eam Seas is my favourite project.

### Elliot Rees (12)
Fleetwood High School, Fleetwood

# Anne Frank

**P** etrified towns and cities
**R** unning away
**I** hid in an attic
**S** hhh... be quiet
**O** nly darkness can be seen
**N** azis attacking
**E** verything is gone
**R** uined lives and millions lost.

## Darcy Hone (12)
Fleetwood High School, Fleetwood

# Bullying

**B** ullying
**U** psetting
**L** oneliness
**L** et down
**Y** ou're not nice
**I** t's not fair
**N** o friends
**G** ood times gone.

## Millie Abram (12)
Fleetwood High School, Fleetwood

# Am I Dead Yet?

I lie in my tomb.
Have I met my doom?
Am I too late?
Have I met my fate?
I feel so blank,
And as still as a plank.
Am I dead yet?

## Delilah Lamb (11)
Fleetwood High School, Fleetwood

# Sketchy? Duo? Never!

Hello and welcome
To the vast world of languages!
Words connect our societies.
If you start learning now, you'll remember forever!
I promise your family will be safe,
We aren't at all sketchy!

Sometimes, people dehumanise others
Simply for how they speak,
But we want to change that,
All in only a few weeks!
As much as people may speculate
About hostages and crime,
We only want to connect,
We aren't sour - despite being lime!

Hello and welcome!
Sign up to Duolingo today!
I, your tutor Duo,
Will lead you all the way!
Connect all around the world
And communicate easily!
I promise your family will be safe,
We aren't at all sketchy!

Little do they know,
*Duo knows where you are.*

Little do you know,
*You'll never be safe, no matter how far you are.*
Little do they know,
*It is a mistake to trust him.*
Little do you know,
You lost your streak!

## Evie Chantler-Harris (12)
Fulston Manor School, Sittingbourne

# OCD

On the outside, I look normal
A friendly family guy
But deep down, there's something awful
With a voice inside my head
I didn't wish for it, no one would
But it hits me before I go to bed.

It happens now and then
The thoughts come and go
Where are my keys?
There they are
Lock the door
Check the van
Other door
You forgot one
We have to leave
They shout at me
Okay it's fine
Now - we can go
No, once more
Lock the door
Check the van
Other door
You forgot one
No. I didn't.

I hop in the car, everyone stares at me
I know, I know, now we can go
They say it's your fault, I agree
*We're always late*, I think to myself
I take a deep breath and watch the world move
I just want to put it high on the shelf.

## Megan Fulton (11)
Fulston Manor School, Sittingbourne

# Eyes Through Alzheimer's

I don't know you
I wish I could
All I know is
I love you.

Who are you?
Not a clue
Whatever is it
Shall I do?

Whatever shall I
Have for dinner?
Have I even
Had my dinner?

What is that thing
Hanging from my wall?
It's too loud and it's
Tall!

What is that?
I don't remember
What is this so-called
... 'pepper'?

Truth and tails never fail...
Truth and tails never fail...

I'll prevail!
What is mail?

I don't know
Who are you?
Please, I'm scared!
Help, it's true!

I am Margaret?
Is that true?
I'm sorry
But do I know you?

## Sophia Seal (13)
Fulston Manor School, Sittingbourne

# The Cutest Pup!

As I wake from my sleep,
The doorbell makes me peep.
I hastily dash to the door,
Waiting for more.
As the door creaks open,
I sit in wait by the gate, sitting and hoping.
As the door stands ajar,
I sit, waiting afar.
As the door opens, I jump up,
I want to be known as the cutest pup.
As I see the faces of the people round,
I can only focus on the surround sound.
The humans are large and warm,
Like the calm before the storm.
I didn't know the storm had come,
As they grab me and wash me anyway.
After the wash, I am left nice and cool,
Cool as a cat riding on a pool.
As I drift off to sleep, I make one final peep,
They say goodbye and take to the cold streets.

**Jacob Nanson (12)**
Fulston Manor School, Sittingbourne

# A Pet

You are my friend
I sleep when I like
I walk when I like
I do anything when I like

I live in your house
I don't pay tax or rent to you
I do my business where I like
You can't stop me doing this

I can run
I can bite
I can climb
I can make noises

I can fart
I can make you mad
I can roll over
I am your pet.

**Rhys Hannam (13)**
Gartree High School, Oadby

# The Truth Behind It All

Here I lie again, my pink king-sized bed,
Wish I'd spoken to her earlier, but I can't now she's dead.
When I try to remember, my mind goes completely black,
My mum gets ready for a show, there are too many, I can't keep track.
Dad's not loyal, he uses his new fame for a girl every day,
But when I ask he denies, it's all he'll ever say.
*I wish I had a life like yours,* my friend blurted out,
I can't wrap my head around it, I'd switch without a doubt.
My parents are repeatedly arguing, over and over again,
Whose side will I take? Should I ask my friend?
Why is there a bruise on your neck? What's going on at home?
I reply with, "Nothing much, just burnt it with a curling comb."
Lies and more lies form along, but you've got money, what could be wrong?
Nobody ever notices, nobody's known for ever so long.
"This is a happy house," we feed to the community and press,
When truly, Dad gets a girl a day, to help him with stress.
After an argument, Mum unexpectedly died,
Was it a coincidence? Or has Dad just lied?
Don't assume someone's life, it's really not cool,
Because you only see what's on the outside, you don't know the truth behind it all…

## Christine Oguno (12)
Nicholas Breakspear Catholic School, St Albans

# Pragmatic Part Of You

*You have been here for what you believe to be a long time*
*But everyone else in this situation*
*Finds it short and defined.*
I feel constrained and want to leave
There is too much going on.
*You may seem ungrateful for their presence*
*And ask what you are doing*
*Your answer will be judged.*
I should wait until the others leave the room
So they do not solely anticipate my return...
Someone has left the room. Should I go?
*You should wait until at least another one leaves*
*So no one accuses you of following them.*
Two others have left, should I -
*You should go, now!*
Quick, before someone returns
I leave the room in a careful manner
So as not to disturb anyone.
*Your expressions may have been deemed weird...*
I feel regret.

## Oliver Richardson (14)
Nicholas Breakspear Catholic School, St Albans

# The Life Of A Tree

When I was younger,
My mother said to me,
You'll grow to be a great tree someday,
But even when you fall,
You'll come back stronger.

Then, I grew big, strong, and tall,
I towered over mosses,
I loomed over foxes,
But the one thing I feared,
Was the dreaded feared by all,
Eliminator of the trees.

I fell that day,
With a crash and a boom,
Scared were the things over which I did loom,
I remembered what my mother said,
I closed my eyes, said goodnight,
At least for now.

After which I did fall,
All the animals large and small,
Wondered what became of a tree like me,
Some said a boat, some said a towering pole,
Some even had the audacity to say an axe.

But what did I become you ask,
A boat, a pole, an axe, a knife or sword,

Would I be large and tall or thin and small,
Would I be smooth or bumpy, hard or soft,
No, I, the grandest tree on Earth,
Would become, a pencil.

## James Lochmuller (12)
Nicholas Breakspear Catholic School, St Albans

# My Day As A Phone

I'm on my counter,
Looking ahead,
I turn next to me,
"She's on the bed,"

It's breakfast time,
And she's tapping my face!
"Stop! Put me down!
Anywhere but this place!"

The morning rolls by,
And it's bread for lunch,
She drops crumbs on me,
A bunch and a bunch!

It's the end of the day,
And my battery's low,
Yet she uses me still,
And uses me so.

And finally,
It's the end of the day,
On my counter,
"I've been put away,"

I feel complete,
I feel good,

'Cause often I feel lonely,
And misunderstood.

This is my place,
This is my time,
To make this very poem,
To make this rhyme.

I must leave you,
Goodbye, cheerio,
I'll see you soon,
But now I must go.

## N'rai Dorsett-Johnson (12)
Nicholas Breakspear Catholic School, St Albans

# The Swim Of His Life

I know what to achieve,
I know how to achieve it,
I just need to execute it.

As I'm doing my final warm-up,
I can hear the announcer,
Counting down to my heat,
Until I hear, "Men's nine and over 200-metre breaststroke, heat seven."

It's my time, my time to qualify for counties,
As I hear the beep for the start,
I push off the block like a rocket,
All my turns are perfect as I'm racing through the water.

I hear the roar from my coach, I need to push more,
I'm pushing myself harder than I ever have,
I touch the wall,
I turn around to look at my time...
'Lane 4: 2:40:371'

I made the time!
Thousands of feelings run through me,
I punch the water in excitement,
I can't believe I made the time.

## Ryan Todd (12)
Nicholas Breakspear Catholic School, St Albans

# The Raven's Tale

The tower was built in ten sixty-six,
When the leadership of England was really quite a mix.
William the Conquerer built this tower and he heard,
That it would always be occupied by a certain bird.
I am one of those birds, both majestic and proud,
The history of our dwelling here has gone far around.
It has been claimed that if we all soar away,
The Kingdom and Tower of London will fall that day.
I do not intend to leave this tower,
But this option has always been my power.
Over three million people come to visit each year,
And all of us will appear.
The Beefeater guards have an important occupation,
Keeping the Crown Jewels and treasure safe for Royalty and Nation.
To be such an important legend truly is amazing,
And this part of history will always need praising.

### Daisy Morgan O'Grady (12)
Nicholas Breakspear Catholic School, St Albans

# Untitled

Social media, a world so vast,
Where teenagers connect and broadcast.
It's a platform where they share their voices,
But its impacts can be a double-edged choice.
Likes and comments, validation sought,
But the pressure to fit in cannot be bought.
Comparison becomes an instant game,
As they strive to perfect their online fame.
Scrolling through feeds for hours on end,
Real-life experiences they may suspend.
But let's not forget the positives it brings,
Connecting with friends and amazing things.
It's important to balance, my friend,
To use social media like it's a positive trend.
Remember you're more than just a profile,
Your worth is not measured by a digital file.
And let social media be just a part,
And not your whole life.

**Skye Minnette (13)**
Nicholas Breakspear Catholic School, St Albans

# Finding Strength

In high school's hustle, feeling kinda small,
New places, new faces, I hit a wall,
Bullies around like the shadows they cast,
Making each day feel like a stormy blast.

In PSHE class, where feelings come alive,
My teacher notices and says, "Let's take a dive,"
You're special, my friend, like a hidden pearl,
In this tough journey, you can conquer the swirl.

After class, in whispers, he shares a tale of his own school day,
How he set sail,
Life's tough, like a puzzle to unfurl,
But remember kiddo, you're special in this world.

Through the taunts and tears,
In the battleground, I find my strength in his words,
I am profound!
In my teacher's support, courage swirls,
I am special, like a hidden pearl.

### Chukwuemeka Ogashi (11)
Nicholas Breakspear Catholic School, St Albans

# I'm Glad That I Tried

I can change everything about me to fit in,
I was ahead of the curve,
It soon shaped into a sphere,
I fell behind on all my friends and ended up here,
At least I'm trying.

I'm still waiting for my pieces to fall into place,
I can bet I can still picture that after too many days,
I sit here looking for a way out of this,
At least I am trying.

I am still standing,
Thinking straight ahead,
I wonder why my brain never means what I actually said,
I can't turn back time,
Why do I dread it?
At least I'm trying.

I changed my mindset,
Not caring what people think,
I know my pieces mended,
It's always been the people that link,
I just had to hold on and find myself a guide,
I'm glad that I tried.

## Lucy Hamilton (11)
Nicholas Breakspear Catholic School, St Albans

# Fast Life

Beneath the helmet's shield, I race the track,
A ballet of speed, where courage won't lack,
Monaco's streets echo with the engines roar,
My heart beats rhythm, chasing dreams galore.

Through twists and turns, a dance of fir and tarmac,
I navigate the circuits, a relentless attack,
In my scarlet hues, my Ferrari paints the day,
Leaving rivals behind, as I find my way.

Raindrops on the visor, a silver cascade,
Yet determination within cannot fade,
I grip the wheel with the spirit of a lion,
In every curve, I find an absolute connection.

Monza's cathedral roars with Tifosi's cheer,
A symphony of passion ringing in my ear,
Charles Leclerc, a name in the wind,
A journey of speed where dreams begin.

**Nicola Pistoia (12)**
Nicholas Breakspear Catholic School, St Albans

# One Lonely Plant

I'm just one lonely plant,
I never have anything to do,
Sometimes I wonder, who would come,
And even hug me too?
It's like I'm non-existent,
Or even a ghost,
But I'm always wondering,
Who loves me the most?

I feel cold and lonely,
There's nothing to do for fun,
No one wanted to be with me,
Not even the sun,
All my roots are broken,
My soil is dry,
So what I'm feeling now is,
When am I going to... bye.

There's always a day,
Why am I still alive?
Even though I'm angry,
I still want to strive,
I don't know the date,
Isn't it the twelfth?
But that doesn't matter,
Because I've got myself.

**Daniel Harris (12)**
Nicholas Breakspear Catholic School, St Albans

# Through My Eyes

**T** hrough my eyes, you all can see
**H** ow tall my neck could possibly be
**R** unning around, I am super speedy
**O** ssicones are my combat weapons, just in case they see me
**U** nder the stars on the Serengeti plains, is where I hunt my prey
**G** entle giant - you may think so, but I'm not scary
**H** ow many teeth? Thirty-two, just like humans.

**M** y spots are extremely unique to me!
**Y** ikes! I am three times taller than adult humans.

**E** yes are key for animals like me
**Y** es, eating is my favourite thing to do
**E** xtinct. Let's hope that never comes to be
**S** ocial creatures are what we are.

## Cameron Mitchell (12)
Nicholas Breakspear Catholic School, St Albans

# A Girl In Gaza

Life has changed forever,
Destruction surrounds me,
Dodging death from the skies,
The feeling of constant hunger.

The air smells of blood and death,
A hard gravel floor, my new mattress,
Red, weeping, tear-stained eyes,
Looking for an end to this.

Yearning for life before,
Luxuries are no more,
Memories not yet faded,
Of a life filled with laughter.

Schoolyards filled with friends,
Tables filled with family,
A future filled with hope,
And dreams to be fulfilled.

In my dreams, this life returns,
In my dreams, this war is over,
In my dreams, peace is everlasting,
In my dreams, Gaza remains my home.

**Tilly Durack Lawlor (11)**
Nicholas Breakspear Catholic School, St Albans

# Not All Monsters Are Scary

Not all monsters are scary,
We might be big,
We might be spiky,
We might have more than two eyes or maybe less,
But I promise we are not all as terrifying as you think.

I'm seven foot tall,
With pink, fluffy fur,
I have huge green eyes and a glistening smile.

I come out at night,
To watch over Ivy,
My four-year-old friend,
Who I look after at night while she sleeps.

Ivy's room is filled with,
Hundreds of teddies and toys,
Fairy lights hanging all around,
Lots of pink shades around the room.

As I said, not all monsters are scary,
We have a soft side,
And we care carefully over the kids.

## Poppy Saunders (13)
Nicholas Breakspear Catholic School, St Albans

# Videogamer

I am Captain Olimar,
Captain of the S.S Dolphin,
I am bringing food to the planet Koppai,
As they are very poor,
I have started my journey to Kappai,
My ship has been hit by an asteroid,
I crash land on an unknown planet,
I search the planet for my ship,
I find it near an onion-like object,
It starts flying and spits out some seeds,
I pluck it and flower-looking people come out, they seem friendly,
I name these people Piknirs,
They help me rebuild my ship,
I am ready to leave when,
I hear my mum calling me,
I guess it is time to stop playing and go back to the real world,
Even if a videogame is similar to the real world.

## Domenico Di Bella (11)
Nicholas Breakspear Catholic School, St Albans

# My Hamster Boo

I was waiting in the cold air.
I was full of surprise when someone wanted me.
I was hiding in the corner of my cage.
I got home and they called me Boo.
My new happy family.

She was curled up in a ball,
She was so excited that I was looking at her,
She was a little snowball,
She was so cute,
She was biting the box,
She was full of joy,
She was running on her wheel when she got in her cage,
She was an explorer,
She jumped at my side,
She was asleep.

Boo, that was her name,
Boo was amazing,
Boo was excited,
Boo was running around her cage,
Boo is a super snowball,
Boo is fascinating.

**Grace Curry (12)**
Nicholas Breakspear Catholic School, St Albans

# Bird

I am a bird, my vision is sharp,
I have a pretty melody, a ring like a harp,
I see a vivid world all around me,
My ears focus on its sound,
The quiet rustle of morning leaves,
A careless whisper in the breeze,
A loud bark from next door,
His paws tap on the kitchen floor,
Near the beach I witness more,
The glistening of the seashore,
All the children having fun,
Playing with their water gun,
A sight of teens skating in the park
Waiting till the sky turns dark,
Parents on their evening date,
I think it's starting to get late...

In my nest, I hush and sleep,
For I know this day will soon repeat.

## Chigozirim Okoh (11)
Nicholas Breakspear Catholic School, St Albans

# The Race

The weather is nice and, oh so bright
I go to the track for my practice laps
I see a friend waiting for me
I say hello as I get ready for my practice laps
Practice is over, and I walk to my mate
Before the race, we talk about the race
The race comes around, and I say, "See you later."
I hop on my bike and see the start flags
Ready, set and go!
I get a good start
I go left to right
Up and down
I get kicked off my bike
I get up and see
What happened
A punch, I give
Next thing, I'm off
And in the blink of an eye
I'm out.

## Alexandru Ghitan (14)
Nicholas Breakspear Catholic School, St Albans

# A Tall Green Life

Grass on the ground,
Stars in the sky,
Is all I've seen,
Throughout my life,
But do not think this is sad,
For these are the best moments that I've ever had,
As I blossom in spring,
And flourish through summer,
The beauty of fall in autumn is like no other,
The cold winter months do not hurt my bark,
Nor the power of love in my big, wooden heart,
So when you walk in the park with your father or mother,
Make sure you show love to my sisters and brothers,
And before you chop us to make your furniture nice,
Listen to the story of my tall green life.

## Finn Flatley (12)
Nicholas Breakspear Catholic School, St Albans

# The Life Of A Dog

In a world of wagging tails and sunny days,
I'm a pup with paws ready for plays.
My fur is rainbow, oh so bright,
I bark with joy morning till night.

Chasing butterflies, what a delight,
Sniffing flowers under the moonlight.
I've got floppy ears that flop, flop, flop,
And a little nose that goes sniff and sop.

Treats and belly rubs, they're so sweet,
They make my world just complete.
Squirrel chasing and muddy paws,
Adventure awaits without a pause.

Late at night, I scruffle and scramble,
Away from a cat, oh, what a shamble!

## Cecilia Turton-Ryz (12)
Nicholas Breakspear Catholic School, St Albans

# Football Vs The Real World

Football, it's a global game,
Loved by all,
But there's still so much pain,
Every week, they take the knee,
In memory of young lives,
So why is knife crime still so rife?
Through the dark and through the light,
The game shines so bright,
They try to make a difference,
Making things right,
But it's still a battle, it's a fight,
It's football vs the real world,
Footballers need to be the voice,
Use their power to help you make the right choice,
Put the knives down and pick up your boots,
Make it to the top,
And never stop.

**Harry Mcmahon (12)**
Nicholas Breakspear Catholic School, St Albans

# Someone's Eyes

In twilight's embrace, shadows dance,
Through weary eyes, life's intricate trance.
A canvas of moments, painted in hues,
Whispers of dreams, as day bids adieu.

Through tear-stained windows, reflections reside,
Echoes of joy and sorrows confide.
Eyes mirror stories, etched in each gaze,
A symphony of emotions, life's endless maze.

In the day's soft glow, a new chapter begins,
Hope blooms afresh, as daylight grins.
Through someone's eyes, a world unfolds,
A face untold, as destiny moulds.

**Angelo Grafanakis (13)**
Nicholas Breakspear Catholic School, St Albans

# The Voice Inside Of You

There's a ghost in this house,
And a startling sound,
A loud snap comes,
And you don't know what from.

You turn around,
Only hearing the sound,
Brain confused,
But heart amused.

The snapping gets closer,
Your mind in a fluster,
What could it be?
And will you make a scene?

Oh you, don't worry,
It's me, no need to hurry,
It's perfectly normal,
Don't need to be formal.

I'm sure I sound familiar,
I'm the voice in your head.

**Kenisha Rebello (14)**
Nicholas Breakspear Catholic School, St Albans

# Dog Alone

Flashing lights, flashing lights,
Oh, how I miss my owner so,
It feels as though,
I'm falling, falling into a deep abyss,
And the deeper it gets, the deeper I miss.

Flashing lights, flashing lights,
Oh, when shall my owner come?
She was in the special some,
I miss the silver hair,
We were such a pair.

Flashing lights, flashing lights,
Oh, how I miss that wrinkled face,
Every day he would embrace,
All alone, I am now,
I will continuously yow,
Waiting, waiting.

**Beatrice Lyden (13)**
Nicholas Breakspear Catholic School, St Albans

# The War I Cannot Bear

I can hear bombs falling
I see bodies everywhere
I can smell rotten decay
This war I can no longer bear.

I walk through my town
Everyone lying dead, gunshots flying through the air
People shouting and screaming
Why is my life so unfair?

I wish I had a lover
I wish I had a future
I wish I had my father
I wish I had my mother.

Why am I alone?
Is anywhere safe? How do I get there?
I feel so scared and angry
Why doesn't the rest of the world care?

**George Marron-Porter (11)**
Nicholas Breakspear Catholic School, St Albans

# A Soldier I Am

The ground swallowed
Dead, wounded soldiers
Ill, bruised, battered, shot dead with lethal weapons
Majority I knew
Some I didn't
Many friends perished but still…
I am a soldier
I have to be strong
I will slay the enemy and will bring
Peace to my country
I shall be in history books
I will be phenomenal
Perhaps people will remember me
Us
I think about my dear wife every night
I yearn to return home and reunite
With my family but for now
A soldier I am.

## Caroline Antwi (11)
Nicholas Breakspear Catholic School, St Albans

# To My Mother

No gift on Earth is greater,
No treasure to claim,
The amusement that I find,
A mother's endless love.

Her battles that she faces,
Provide her strength and confidence.
The clouds draw her image,
The angels gift me from the sky.

The light that surrounds
The darkness,
The guide to a tremendous passion,
Like a bright and shining star.

Of all the special joys in life,
The extensive and slight,
The prominent one
Is a mother's endless love.

**Harry Brandon Mukesha (14)**
Nicholas Breakspear Catholic School, St Albans

# Brain Or Heart

It's a never-ending fight
Brain versus heart
Which one should take the lead?
The brain is logical
But the heart is full of passion
The brain has wisdom and knowledge
But the heart tells us how to love
But we need to agree that they are both crucial
Without the heart, the brain wouldn't work
Without the brain, the heart wouldn't work
The two tie in the fight
You need both to be complete
The brain and the heart
One's got the keys
The others got the safe.

**Gilda Kyeremeh (13)**
Nicholas Breakspear Catholic School, St Albans

# Day In His Life

I get out of bed,
A very tough day ahead,
A long day of school.

When I get to school,
My friends are very cool,
But another long day at school.

The day is almost over,
And I can't wait to roll over,
In the blazing sun.

Me and my sister on the bus,
She is always making a big fuss,
When we arrive home.

She goes straight on her phone,
In her room all alone,
She goes to sleep
And the cycle repeats,
Another long day of school.

**Hannah Guerrini (13)**
Nicholas Breakspear Catholic School, St Albans

# The Game

**T** errible death,
**H** unger of poor children,
**E** qual rights to the districts.

**G** o home,
**A** westruck by what the audience sees,
**M** issing family,
**E** xquisite food for the winner when they go home.

**M** arvellous outfits to show off,
**A** ching pain of losers' families,
**K** illing because of cheating,
**E** vil, the game makers are malicious,
**R** ebel against Snow,
**S** tarved to death.

## Holly Vanderhoven (12)
Nicholas Breakspear Catholic School, St Albans

# NFS

There I was in the car,
The roaring car,
The fastest car,
Off we went.
Then I heard something,
It was Dad, but I couldn't make out...
Oh no! Tree, tree, tree.
That was close!

I got this
Zipping it, round one
Heard the crowd shouting my name
Close chase
Chase and then I...
Slid out, Mayday help!
I can't help but yelp
Oh no, I felt
As loud as a lion
As hot as the sun.
The car blew me a goodbye...
In flames!

**Salman Taman (13)**
Nicholas Breakspear Catholic School, St Albans

# Beyond

This lonely sea has always appealed to me,
So fascinating and free,
That I envision what lies beyond this horizon,
To understand,
It must feel like a whisper,
Of comfort to my ear,
Tender and mild,
I must silence the leap of my heart to hear,
What doesn't thrive in the present,
Remains untouched,
My soul,
Still,
Is yet to be found.

In such immensity, my thought is drowned,
And it is pleasant to be shipwrecked,
In this sea.

### Natalia Di Girgenti (12)
Nicholas Breakspear Catholic School, St Albans

# The Life Of A Squirrel

When I wake up I feel all scruffy,
I scratch myself so I don't feel fuzzy,
As I clamber up trees,
I can feel the breeze,
The wind is rustling the leaves,
And shaking my knees,
As often as I come to run,
The enemy will always come,
I get chased by the crow,
But it is far too slow,
After a busy day's work,
And making the crows go berserk,
I walk along the fence keeping my balance,
And run up the old oak straight to my palace.

**Erik Verboom (11)**
Nicholas Breakspear Catholic School, St Albans

# Perspective Of A Timid Year Seven

In a big school,
With a big site,
Coming to school
Gave Gabriella a big fright.

Chatters and whispers,
And large crowded classes,
Only one thing gave goosebumps to her
Was older students just walking in laughter.

Pushing and shoving made her feel so small,
But one of the elder
Scared her most of all.
Mitchell Sanhall.

Grabbing and shouting,
Shoving and growling.
She wanted to curl up and cry.

**Pippa Mann (11)**
Nicholas Breakspear Catholic School, St Albans

# Tree

I stand tall,
No one is as strong as me.
I shall not fall,
Even if I am slanted at a 45 angle degree.

My brothers and sisters normally get chopped down,
But I am the firmest of all of them.
I deserve a crown,
After all, I have the strongest stem.

My strength is a human weakness,
Over time I will rot,
But that won't be soon because of my uniqueness,
Anyway, the very sad part is that I'll soon be forgotten.

## Michael Ojo (11)
Nicholas Breakspear Catholic School, St Albans

# Time To Stop

*Tony, it's time to stop*
I gaze across the Octagon to be met by menacing, white, glazed eyes
Pure fear holds me back,
Terrified to move a muscle.
The iron bars of the cage grip me fiercely
*Tony, it's time to stop*
The crowd's booming, deafening noise and cries put me in a daze
A direct head kick hurls itself in my direction as I
Swiftly but narrowly evade it.
*Tony, it's time to retire.*

## Oliver Bradshaw (14)
Nicholas Breakspear Catholic School, St Albans

## Isak's Insanity

Oh Isak, what a talent
Dancing with the ball
At his feet through the
Defences, oh how scared
They are. He's played
In Spain and he made
His mark then he
Left to join the
Magpies. He is
Tall and agile
His determination
Is beyond amazing
A future legend
We all know.
So let's cheer for Isak
As he continues to
Grow and claim his
Fame. The gifted
Giant with more to
Come.

**Marcel Giorko (11)**
Nicholas Breakspear Catholic School, St Albans

## Benevolence

Giving out love and never receiving,
Stops many from no longer caring or believing,
They give up on others and start to expect,
They lose all of their empathy, sympathy and respect,
That's why benevolent words are the best things to say,
So others spread your benevolence to make someone's day,
But Michael has even experienced this and never stopped giving,
His outgoing heart keeps singing and living.

### Michael Oliver (12)
Nicholas Breakspear Catholic School, St Albans

# Dreaming

When it is winter Mum wants it to snow
If it does, her eyes start to glow
As she digs into the cold snow
She builds a snowman
But she gets too cold
So she heads inside
And drinks her hot chocolate
By the warm fire
Dreaming that it would be summer
Sitting on the beach
Sipping a glass of Fanta
Then, swimming in the clear blue Mediterranean Sea
But she realised she was just dreaming.

## Heidi Rouse (11)
Nicholas Breakspear Catholic School, St Albans

# Animal

Where you see fun,
I see intruding.
Where you see entertainment,
I see suffering.

Stop putting us in cages,
For people to visit your zoo.
Teach your children,
Out point of view.

Let us roam free,
Just like you.
If tables were to turn,
What would you do?

I would set you free,
I would be your friend,
We can share the world,
A life well spent.

### Eric Balan (13)
Nicholas Breakspear Catholic School, St Albans

# Through Their Eyes, Past Their Lies

Through their eyes, past their lies...
A wall of demise.
Failure and loss.
Is a heavy cost.
Road of temptation.
Giving in and losing.
Going through the constant abusing.
Garden of shadows.
Once met.
With a load of regret.
A wall of lies.
The answers that we seek.
To which we will never meet.
Bell of violence.
The last resort of much.
But not the end of such.

**Ollie Brandle (14)**
Nicholas Breakspear Catholic School, St Albans

# Sapphire's Dream

The moon shone at midnight
So all the stars could see
Glistening in the moonlight, it was like it was born to be seen
As round as an ox
As sly as a fox
It surreptitiously passed by
As the sun was glimmering
It had appeared to the moon
Why was he not as known?
Then again
It was like Sapphire's dream
Nobody knew
Why he was suspiciously
Never to be seen.

## Mia Lamptey (11)
Nicholas Breakspear Catholic School, St Albans

# Enough Chaos

Extremely tired of hackers
On you, they can place trackers
They will always hate
Just to hack your mate
They will just seem nice
But they will make you put your phone in rice
You will think they love
But they will make you look like a dove
They will ruin your life
Virtually stab you with a knife
There's nothing much to do
Not even a virtual zoo.

## Jakub Ostrowski (14)
Nicholas Breakspear Catholic School, St Albans

# A Wandering Cat

I'm a cat,
I don't do much,
I sleep all the time,
I'm never home,
Until my owners get home.

I'm a cat,
I don't do much,
I chill in a bush all day,
I'm never home,
Until that door opens.

I'm a cat,
I don't play with toys,
I scratch sofas,
I'm never home,
Until the key is in that door.

## Alexander Mazoruk (13)
Nicholas Breakspear Catholic School, St Albans

# The Striker!

Through his eyes, I saw the harsh football striker,
Sprinting towards me through his eyes,
I felt pressured into making a bad decision.
Through his eyes, I tried making a prediction on his next move,
Through his eyes, he had a much higher advantage than me,
Through his eyes, I was extremely focussed,
Finally, I got my win, I won the ball!

## Charlie Burns (11)
Nicholas Breakspear Catholic School, St Albans

# Refugee

No home, no love
But a very hard shove
No clothes, no food
I am as dead as I'll ever be.

Nothing awaits me
Neither at home or somewhere else
Refugees come to thee, fear, horror and flee.

Now I know how much refugees have to suffer
Why am I the child that always weeps?
No sleep, no love but a hard shove.

**Ruairí Hickey (13)**
Nicholas Breakspear Catholic School, St Albans

## Is This The End?

The train leaves the station,
I watch my mother cry,
I hope that wasn't the last time I will see her,
My siblings cuddled into my side,
Their eyes are wet,
We already miss Mother,
She's all alone,
Father's at war,
We haven't seen him for three months,
I hope he can save us,
Will this be the end?

### Ellie Davies (11)
Nicholas Breakspear Catholic School, St Albans

# Escape

Take courage,
Be brave,
And drive ahead,
Start where you stand,
To build a,
Better life,
With the people,
You love and,
Forget the past,
And focus on,
The future ahead,
Of you, to start,
A new beginning,
With your dreams,
Ahead of you waiting,
For you to come,
Never give up.

## Pulane Urneh (13)
Nicholas Breakspear Catholic School, St Albans

# Titanic

I can see your smile from a mile away,
I hear your voice even though it was not my choice,
I can feel your love inside me without you I feel empty,
I gave you my heart so we don't feel apart,
When I was drawn I felt a thorn,
From the rose that I chose,
This will end here,
Forever you will be my dear.

**Ruby Martin (12)**
Nicholas Breakspear Catholic School, St Albans

# Books

I can make you snore when I am a chore
I have many worlds for you to explore

I'm active and fun, you can't be done!
'Cause when you pick me up, I am so much fun!

I can be small or tall, short or big,
Whatever size, I'm the next big thing.

### Erin Dunnigan (12)
Nicholas Breakspear Catholic School, St Albans

# All Their Eyes

The crowd roared with passion
They shouted my name
All I could see
Were people here for me.

The music boomed
The lights flashed
Phone lights waved
They were ecstatic.

I riled them up
Now all eyes were on me
All of their eyes.

**Nathaniel Hettiarachchi (14)**
Nicholas Breakspear Catholic School, St Albans

# A Phone

Every day, I want to look at you,
All the time you ring,
You can play all day,
And it will last,
Chatting all day every day,
Get what you want,
Going through all your posts,
Taking photos every day,
Waking me up to get to school.

## Niall Hubbard (11)
Nicholas Breakspear Catholic School, St Albans

## Beast Of Generosity

**M** y face drives them crazy,
**R** acing to reach me.

**B** ut they mean no harm,
**E** njoying my gifts,
**A** nd I look around at them,
**S** miling at me,
**T** he person who made their day.

### Ryan Shine (13)
Nicholas Breakspear Catholic School, St Albans

# Dusty The Dreadful

**D** angerous and disturbing
**U** nderstands how much she annoys
**S** teals my attention
**T** ries to intimidate me
**Y** our overall favourite...

## Francesca Avila (11)
Nicholas Breakspear Catholic School, St Albans

# The Pain Of World War Two

**W** e were dragged away from our homes
**O** nly to be forced to fight for our country
**R** anked in lines and led to war
**L** eaving our beloved families
**D** ying soldiers lying on the floor in pain.

**W** aiting to be set free to see our families again
**A** bout 45% of people have died so far
**R** unning away from rivals, nearly being killed.

**T** errified, worried, scared, I fear I'll never see my kids again.
**W** on't give up until this war is over.
**O** nly to realise I will never see my family again.

## Lily Dauncey (13)
Poole High School, Poole

# Why Am I Like This?

D o people disgrace me?
I am constantly left in shame
R eading your expression
T empestuous anger swells
Y ou must stop stepping on me

D on't be a pushover
O r you'll end up not free
O riginally, I was scared
R ecently, I will fight
M any people stepped on me
A nd that is just not right
T o all the people who stepped on me, I will put up a fight.

## Erin Harker (12)
Poole High School, Poole

# My Cats

Mouse eater,
Frog killer,
Hungry eater,
Lazy thing,
Fighter,
Have a brother,
Crash,
Meow,
Meow,
Like a lion,
Jump to high five,
Roll over like a dog,
Acts like a dog,
Hiss,
Meow,
Mouse eater,
Frog killer,
Follower,
Hungry eater,
I am a cat.

## Olivia Young (13)
Poole High School, Poole

## The Alleyway Cat

**A** cat is agile,
**L** onely and fragile.
**L** ooking for mischief,
**E** arnest, but always called a thief.
**Y** earning for adventure,
**W** e will never surrender.
**A** n alleyway cat,
**Y** ou can be sure of that.

### Jasmine Dodgson (12)
Poole High School, Poole

# I Am Batman

I am the Dark Knight
Gotham City is my home
I use my fists to fight
I work alone.

I work late hours
I am Gotham City's only fighter
Perching on towers
Solving riddles and fighting a Joker

Because I am Batman.

## Aaron King (12)
Poole High School, Poole

# Untitled

I'm so tired.
I am wringed out
Towel on
The edge of a rack
Sitting?
No, hanging from
Neck.
Exhausted.
Too tired to even move.
I shouldn't complain,
At least it's warm
Between
Six and seven
Also between
Seven and ten.
I'm drained, all
My enjoyment
Gone.
Time ticks as I dry
On the radiator
From six to seven, seven to ten.
Six seven, seven ten.
I wait.
I hang.
I'm tired again.
I would cry

But I used my tears
On miscommunications
With the faucet to my left.
I would sleep
But I get no peace
From the whirring of the
Radiator.
I'm so tired all the time.
"Go to bed" they cry
But I can't, I'm busy
Waiting for the heat
To engulf me,
"Take a break" they plead,
I can't...
I'm so tired of this life.

**Reo Warwick (16)**
Queen Mary's College, Basingstoke

# Cannae

If Steel and Scarlet through grasses wades,
The heavy tread of Roman Legions now
Is heard. A savage smile from Barca's lips pervades.
My eyes this see: his mien, an ancient row.

"Oh come on, Varro!" Impatient moans
pervade. Not even, reckon I, shall Rome's
Hands' tread so heavy to auger their groans...
Before us scything us like at the grain of their homes.

The farmers, stirred from soil known, toil
Away their freedoms fiercely persevering
Yet we, we are Spaniards, Gauls; on soil
Foreign must we be here lab'ring, slaving?

Punic footmen pounding over plains
As Roman dreams... lie in chains?

## Henry Haddock (16)
Rainey Endowed School, Magherafelt

# Tsunami

The warm sand tickled my toes and I admired the waves come crashing down,
Life was perfect just the way it was,
Until I noticed that the ocean began to run
Away like it wanted me to play tag,
A screeching alarm began and everyone started to panic,
In the distance, was a horrifying over ten-foot wave, coming towards me,
My heart skipped five beats and I stood up and sprinted as fast as possible,
But it was too late,
The freezing wave engulfed me as I gasped for air,
The pain slapped me around the face,
Darkness was all I could see and I
Felt like the world had just stabbed me in the back,
Would I survive?

**Tillie Orton (12)**
Roundhill Academy, Thurmaston

# Ocean View

In the distance a cherry-red boat approaches.
As it strides through the water shrieks of terror are emitted.
As the sun falls, bright lights appear from the ship.
Eventually, the ship leaves the horizon.

Soon dark storm clouds start to loom.
After heavy rain falls and the wind blows.
The wind crashes against the water and havoc erupts.
Soon after chaos and the storm dies down.

Later a small voice approaches from the distance.
It comes from a person on a small plank of wood.
Soon the horn of a large ship can be heard.
Eventually, the person manages to get on board the vessel.

**Manjot Singh (12)**
Roundhill Academy, Thurmaston

# Sitting By Mat...

I was just a cute pup when we first met,
I loved you from the start,
You picked me up and took me home,
And placed me in your heart.

The good times we had,
We shared all life could throw,
There was something missing in your home.

The sun will rise and will find your eyes,
You loved me more than your own,
Our memories are golden like me,
The movie nights when we cuddled till the moon disappeared.

Sharing some secrets that only you knew,
We played under the forbidden tree until dawn came around.

## Maya Patel (11)
Roundhill Academy, Thurmaston

# The Forgotten Bracelet

War and conflict,
People dying,
Refugees crying.
I hide with my friend
Close together and sobbing too,
The wind howled like a wolf at noon.
Earlier that day, we made bracelets for the refugees,
For friendship of course.
Escaping on boats for safety,
Unfortunately, we were on different boats.
"We've been sailing for hours," I moaned,
I screamed in horror at what I saw,
The friendship bracelet I made.
Bobbing up and down in the water,
Covered in blood.

## Charlie Bailey (12)
Roundhill Academy, Thurmaston

# Refugees

R efugees are always misunderstood
E yes staring looking at what is happening to our country
F ighting, bombing, and crying of my mum and sister. Help us!
U nder my straight face, I'm crying too
G rasping my mother's hand, hoping just hoping
"E veryone stay inside!" says the television
E yes just staring at what our country has become
S ilenced by war, I realise we have to leave this country I grew up in. Why am I here? Just why?

**Isla-Mae Simpson (11)**
Roundhill Academy, Thurmaston

# Through The Eyes Of An Astronaut

As I face the darkness of space,
I see the Earth and the whole human race,
I think about what we are and what we can be,
As I stare at beautiful forests and the delicate sea,
I keep staring and I can see
Deforestation and pollution in the sea.
Wildfires beneath me,
Earthquake cracks,
What are we leaving in our tracks?
What are we doing to our delicate world,
Makes me sad and makes me cross,
Society is chasing the lowest cost,
And if we're not careful the world will be lost.

## Emma Limb (11)
Roundhill Academy, Thurmaston

# The Very Strange School!

She goes to a very strange school,
In the classroom, there is a pool.
Her headteacher came
To present his fame.
Then he stupidly ran into a wall.

She goes to a very strange school,
They always have to stand on a stool.
The teacher was so dumb,
He cut off his thumb.
Now they all think he is very cool.

She goes to a very strange school,
They aren't allowed to play with a ball,
So they tell the teacher,
That he is a creature.
How dare he be so cruel!

**Asha Lakhani (11)**
Roundhill Academy, Thurmaston

# Forgotten

How happy I was
How joyful I seemed
I would never forget what it meant to me.

The splash of colour
My bristles getting fuller
Now, I'm lying down the drain,
Hoping someday…
I will be used again.

Now I'm lying in a pot while my friends glide with glee…
I will never forget how much it meant to me.

Someday, I think of how I would feel,
Someday, I think of what could be real,
Creating art
To not be apart…
As I drown myself in my sorrows…

**Anika Khushalbhai (12)**
Roundhill Academy, Thurmaston

# Through Their Eyes

As I swim around in my tank
The water is weird,
Until I see a huge beard.
I swim around terrified,
Oh, it was just my owner.
As food rains down,
I quickly swim around,
Catching every piece in my mouth,
I go back to my huge big house.
As I close my eyes and sleep.
I feel Earth's creek.
I fall asleep in the moss.

**Keelan Brown (11)**
Roundhill Academy, Thurmaston

# A Cat's Life

Goes outside
Rains all night
Left outside
Cries hungry, cold as ice
They play with the dog
Forgot I'm alive
Gets left inside
Shoes away
I cry all day
I'm not the favourite anymore
They don't want to play
Pulled around
I left the house
Gone forever
They look for me
I cry in the rain day and night
They find me under a tree
I'm happy and loved once more.

## Connie McDonald (11)
Roundhill Academy, Thurmaston

# Through Their Eyes

What do they see
When they look at me?

Guns drawn and heads up high
Do they see a coward? Or
Do they see a hero?
My fear drops from high to zero.

What do they see
When they look at me?

As I run toward them from
The front line
And scream out loud
Victory is mine!

**Kyle Smith (12)**
Roundhill Academy, Thurmaston

# In Her Eyes

In her eyes,
if you cried, she would hold you.
In her eyes,
if you called, she would answer.
In her eyes,
if you needed to talk, she would listen.
In her eyes,
she would always be there,
but if she needed you,
you wouldn't answer her calls.
If she needed you, you would never sit
and listen.
If she needed you,
you were never there.

## Mia Brookes (12)
Roundhill Academy, Thurmaston

# Through The Eyes Of War

I am war,
I attack every single country I see in my eyes,
I am evil in my eyes,
I am very jealous of people loving and caring
About the others who wouldn't fight for our country,
In my eyes I see people caring
As the war has got harder,
Harder with every attack we all go through.

**Brooke Simmons (12)**
Roundhill Academy, Thurmaston

# My Cricket Bat

The grip is torn off
The wood is chipped and damaged
The bat is covered in hardball marks

When I hit it for six
The ball goes high in the air
I do it again but it breaks!

That was my only bat
The one with all the autographs
My opponents laugh.

**Rikin Thanki (11)**
Roundhill Academy, Thurmaston

# Dance Of Delight: A Whimsical Journey

In a land where laughter dances on air
A tale unfolds, whimsical and rare
Under the sun's cheerful glow
I embark on a journey, letting laughter flow
With a skip in my step, a twinkle in my eye
Over the vast, endless, cerulean sky
Gather around dear friends, and let the adventure start
In this theatre of life playing my part
A canvas of moments splashed with bright colours of happiness
Oh what a sight! I'm the conductor of laughter's grand symphony
Notes of merriment, a joyful cacophony through meadows of giggles
Where wildflowers bloom
In the dance of happiness, dispelling all gloom
I chase butterflies of whimsy, so free
A protagonist is me
Climbing hills of humour, reaching the summit, high
Surfing on waves of jest beneath the azure sky
In the comedy of life, a stand-up routine in which the comedian is crafting the scene
Beside the laughter river I take a stroll
With every chuckle life beckons whole
Skipping stones of joy on the water's embrace
I am the poet narrating this joyful space

Through time's tunnels where echoes resound in memory
Carnival happiness is found; architect of dreams
Whimsical and grand building joyous castles of golden sand
Here's to adventure, laughter and play in life's story
I'm the lead today with a heart full of mirth
A spirit untamed in this tale I am named.

**Serena Ayube (13)**
Stopsley High School, Luton

# The Dark Night Returns

The dark awakes
The night shakes
As you venture through the storm.

Night falls but you rise
As you laugh
Watching a dog play with its toy balls.

The storm screams
When the light shines
As you care for the dreams in your mind.

It's in your hands
So show it to all
Go outside
And have a ball.

You approach the finish line
But not yet anyway
You realise it's your time

Day is almost here
When darkness comes
The dark night will return...

**Lilley-Mae Ryn-Wild (12)**
Swanwick Hall School, Alfreton

# The Life Of A Sperm Whale

My life is over, that is true,
But now it's time for the brand new.
I saw my pod, slaughtered and killed,
I was alone, and sad; I was chilled.
The humans' hearts are all so small,
They didn't take one, they took all!
Years later I was out and about,
I went up to the surface to spout.
I saw a boat with a happy lad,
He seemed so happy, I couldn't be mad,
He was called David Attenborough; I never knew the guy,
He went up and chipped me, I never knew why.
People are ecstatic when they see me,
I didn't get it, I was just being me.
I guess humans aren't so bad,
Now it's time to see my mum and dad.

## Mergen Ariunzol (11)
The Heys School, Prestwich

# Where's My Forest?

I am Little John,
My family is gone,
Where are the trees?
The bugs and the bees?

Monkey mum and monkey dad,
Was I ever that bad?
The humans came,
With axes and flame.

No more fun,
My house is done,
I miss my best friend,
And the forest we'd defend.

My time has come,
Just like my mum,
My final stand,
To defend my land.

The humans are here,
I'm starting to fear,
How can I defend?
I'll meet my end.

They took the trees,
The bugs and the bees,

Because of them, my family is gone,
And there is no more Little John.

## Nate Sloan (12)
The Heys School, Prestwich

# Untitled

Humans suck
They use my home for their books
Ruining my life
Their bloody scream making knives
And even though I lost my home
I stay as there is nowhere else to go
My house toppled over that one time
Those luscious green leaves no longer lime

I watch no longer from the trees
The horrible things I have seen
It all makes we want to cry
Saying it'll be okay is a lie
Different types of life among me
My beautiful house turned to ten
No one left
Just little cold Jimmy.

**Nnenna Okocha (11)**
The Heys School, Prestwich

# Through Their Eyes

My eyes flicker into life
A faint flurry of blinking
As I adjust to the piercing white light
And when I can
I gaze around at my feeble, delicate body
Which feels strangely foreign
As though it is not my own
I'm cradled in the arms of a towering giant
Not an uncomfortable experience, but
But this is my reality now
A weak, fragile creature
For now.

I shall grow
I hope
Prosper
And grow into a being akin to those holding me
Become all I can.

And grow I did, blossoming into a young adult,
So similar to them
But so different
I am so beautifully unique
So me in every sense.

Sometimes it can be an isolating experience
But only when you interpret it as such
As outlook truly does influence more than you'd think.

I stumble through life,
Simply putting one foot in front of the next
And hope everything is okay
As I grow more lucid about the situations around me though
I realise
Everyone is doing the same
Blagging their way through existence

As this is everybody's first time too.

### Jack Rigby (15)
The Peterborough School, Peterborough

# Through My Mother's Eyes

One day, my heart split into two,
Not in a bad way, to say the truth.
A new creature in my arms... For God's sake, his face gave me a bright new sight,
His sweet smile makes my skin crawl but in a good way.
Soon, he grew to be a young child.
First day of school, my creature looked nervous, but he soon saw his school as something precious,
And then, at the next moment, he was already making his own decisions,
He seems to want liberty, but the world is dangerous, and full of insecurity.
I'm trying to protect him,
But he seems to see me as the main danger at the moment,
But now, my creature has got his first job...
What a confusing moment; he was ten just a second ago,
I wonder how he grew into this independent man in a breath ago.
But now, he looks ready for the world, ready to start his own family,
That creature that I love,
As finally, my mystery is solved.
How maternity changed me,
Will soon turn him like me...
And it all feels like yesterday.

**Princess Adora Aiyeki Uyinmwen (15)**
The Salesian Academy Of St John Bosco, Bootle

# Selfishness

Once upon a time, there was a man,
He was a very social and kind man,
He decided to test his luck to see if he was a lucky man,
He went into a shop and bought a ticket,
Not just any ticket, a lottery ticket,
He went to sleep and the next day woke up as a lucky man,
The man's luck was very good,
The man went out to buy a coat with a hood,
Then he saw a shop with some sweets,
And decided to get something to eat,
Then he saw a drink shop ahead,
But decided to get a milkshake instead,
Then he turned selfish,
And shared his money with no one,
He started to lose friends,
And he liked no one in the end,
He decided to go for some ice cream,
But when he walked in, everyone ran out and screamed,
Then he realised what he'd done,
And what he had become.

## Jay Keir (12)
The Salesian Academy Of St John Bosco, Bootle

# My Dog Is...

My dog is...
Small and fluffy,
Super cuddly,
Sweet and lovely,
My favourite buddy.
She has soft fur with big ears,
Chocolate brown eyes,
And the cutest of smiles,
She loves going on walks,
But hates having baths.

She loves walks in the lake,
And loves it when I bake,
Especially when it's dog cake.

She hates cats,
But not the ones wearing hats,
She likes to sit on her mats,
Watching bats.

My dog is the best!
She's small and fluffy,
Super cuddly,
Sweet and lovely,
My favourite buddy!

**Leticia Frozi Bona (13)**
The Salesian Academy Of St John Bosco, Bootle

# Through Their Eyes

As cold as snow,
The body is soon to be found,
The body is as green as an apple,
Scratching his head as if it's fur,
Suddenly, finding a scent to beware of,
The smell is worse than a rotting corpse,
He was soon to find out,
As he walked around the school it was getting closer,
The smell getting worse,
It was found, a body rotting,
More flies than people,
The smell was getting worse,
Fingerprints on the rotting body,
He was soon to find out who committed the murder.

## Charlie Mullin (12)
The Salesian Academy Of St John Bosco, Bootle

# Two

Two houses, two homes,
Two kitchens, two phones,
Two couches where I lay,
Two places that I stay,
Moving, moving here and there,
From Monday to Friday, I'm everywhere,
Don't get me wrong, it's not that bad,
But often times it makes me sad.

And then one day, someone walks into your life,
A total stranger and they become so important to you,
And while you've known them such a short time,
You feel you have loved them for a lifetime.

### Marie Didiova (12)
The Salesian Academy Of St John Bosco, Bootle

# Royal

- **R** ight through my eyes, you would see just how horrid my life can be.
- **O** nly when you know how difficult it truly is, then you can judge me.
- **Y** ou claim royals have it easy but you don't know what we go through, you don't know what we see.
- **A** nd if you could, trust me now, you wouldn't trust us, no.
- **L** et me warn you, for it is disturbing. Royals' lives aren't easy and someday you will see.

## Isabella Flynn-Farley (12)
The Salesian Academy Of St John Bosco, Bootle

# Through Their Eyes

'Run, run as fast as you can
You can't catch me, I'm the Gingerbread Man'
I run high and low
To get away from this awful fellow
I can't fly or climb
I am worth a dime
I don't know why he's chasing me
It feels selected if you ask me
I came out the oven freshly baked
But I can't swim in any lake
I will talk to you later
This man is a bad baker...
Gingerbread Man.

### Jack Mullin (12)
The Salesian Academy Of St John Bosco, Bootle

# The End Of Peace

Devils shared levels,
They lived on ground,
Where humans were bound,
Angels occasionally got found.

Although angels lived far,
They forced people into tar,
It became a law, so they began war,
Humans won.

Devils forced them below,
Angels went above,
Humans received doves,
Humans became alone,
Only one home,
They wanted the others back,
The answer became no.

## Fiona Raduta (12)
The Salesian Academy Of St John Bosco, Bootle

# Motherhood

M aking mistakes along the way,
O nly if she knew how to raise another life,
T ime, she never had enough of.
H ow was she going to pick up the role of a mother?
E very second counted.
R eminiscing her own childhood.
H ow was she going to cope?
O lder now, the child was.
O ver the mother, she was. Fed up.
D ays passing by, motherhood over in the blink of an eye.

### Caitlyn Bailey (14)
The Salesian Academy Of St John Bosco, Bootle

# When Will Summer Come?

The winter wind makes everyone freeze,
Whilst all are longing for that summer breeze,
When will we get that summer sun?
How long until all our beach fun?
Everyone wants to get away on a plane,
But for now, all we have is rain,
We all get stuck in the snow,
When we want to hear the river flow,
Everyone loves to have a ball,
But just for now, the snow will still fall.

## Ava Brady (13)
The Salesian Academy Of St John Bosco, Bootle

# Untitled

As the sun set at around 7pm, I went past the woods.
No one could quite understand why or how it was haunted.
So I wanted to check.
The woods gave off an eerie feeling and a shiver down my spine that felt like someone stabbed me.
Why would this be?
I could hear the wolves howling.
And the wind whistling against the trees.
With the dead of silence.

**Lily Grace Richman**
The Salesian Academy Of St John Bosco, Bootle

# When The Poppies Grew

The bombs, they blew
The bricks, they flew.
They began a war
Did anyone know what for?
The poppies rose,
The statues of soldiers pose.
Then the caskets close...

Blood red poppies,
Grew from the war ground,
They soon became found,
But bodies also lay above,
The angels, they sent a dove,
This was to show all their love.

## Analishia Hessing McGinn (12)
The Salesian Academy Of St John Bosco, Bootle

# Untitled

**F** amous for scoring goals.
**O** verwhelming, can't miss a shot.
**O** ffside, a love/hate relationship.
**T** ime, 90 minutes to win.
**B** all, the object of the game.
**A** nger, someone hurts someone.
**L** oved, they love their team.
**L** ife, football is life.
**E** verton, a cool team.
**R** ivalry - Everton Vs Liverpool.

## Declan Parker (14)
The Salesian Academy Of St John Bosco, Bootle

## On The Beach

**B** y the shore, I can see the waves passing by calmly.
**E** very person I walk past has an ice lolly.
**A** s I see the turtles wandering back into the clear sea peacefully.
**C** ool breeze suddenly hits my face.
**H** owever, I can see the sunset going darker and darker as I step into the sea.

### Lily Benton Newman (12)
The Salesian Academy Of St John Bosco, Bootle

# School

Every day is the same,
Just like the last.
Sometimes, I wish,
I could go back to the past.
Back then, it was all calm and nice,
But now I hardly want to go back more than twice.
Oh some days, we can go out in the sun,
But when it's winter, we can't go out and have some fun.

## Tyler Draper (12)
The Salesian Academy Of St John Bosco, Bootle

# Through Their Eyes
*Taylor Swift*

On stage shining so bright
Like a star in the night
With music like magic, so loud
Captivating the crowd

In a glittering outfit, singing and dancing
With my performance enhancing
Whilst lyrics touch hearts and melodies soar
Taylor Swift, a legend, forevermore.

## Laila McDonough (12)
The Salesian Academy Of St John Bosco, Bootle

# From The Eyes Of A Villager

**R** oyalty is on its way,
**O** pen hearts are all that's left,
**Y** our heart is all they want,
**A** king needs my heart,
**L** ife is gone,
**T** o love the kingdom, they need your heart,
**Y** ou'll regret coming here; take that from me.

## Mylie Walsh (12)
The Salesian Academy Of St John Bosco, Bootle

# A Field Of Flowers

Standing tall and lean
Waving to the green
Listening to the trees
Feeling the warm breeze
Lying on the grass
Still like glass
Cars going by
While I lie
Same old every day
Till I am old and grey
Blowing to and fro
Watching the time go.

**Emilee Stevens (12)**
The Salesian Academy Of St John Bosco, Bootle

# Newborn Baby

When you're first born,
You're so tiny like a beautiful sunflower trying to grow
And when everyone sees you all these hearts grow
Because they're full of love and joy.
Even when you were in their belly
You start kicking, they can feel your little feet.

**Mary Robinson (15)**
The Salesian Academy Of St John Bosco, Bootle

# A Terror's Call To War

In sunlight's absence,
I lay motionless.
I rue the path my leader motioned us.
Aching and maimed, lay bathing in sorrow,
For I had become a husk so hollow.
The beats and the whips, I endured it all,
All of this to bring one force's fall.

**Caiden Molloy (13)**
The Salesian Academy Of St John Bosco, Bootle

# London Is Falling Down

**L** oud crashes
**O** bserving the ruins from above
**N** o more London
**D** ead bodies scattered around the city
**O** ld monuments turned into rubble
**N** ever to be seen again.

The point of view is from an RAF pilot.

## Carmen Roscoe (13)
The Salesian Academy Of St John Bosco, Bootle

# A Student's Perspective

**T** eaching us things we don't understand.
**E** verything we do is wrong.
**A** lways shouting.
**C** an't understand children's point of view
**H** elping but not enough.
**E** verything is our fault.
**R** epeating everything they say.

## Emma-Jayne Smith (15)
The Salesian Academy Of St John Bosco, Bootle

# The Darkness

The dark, misty clouds came upon me
While the rain was falling on me, I got wet.
The rain was heavy
The clouds went heavy
A person came and said,
"Do you want to come to the park?"
The dogs would bark.

## Thomas Meath (12)
The Salesian Academy Of St John Bosco, Bootle

# Trapped!

**D** ead soldiers lying on the floor,
**Y** oung and trapped inside their young minds,
**I** magine a place with suffering and regret.
**N** ot enough time to run,
**G** ot to get out before the shots go *bang!*

## Sophie Duckworth (14)
The Salesian Academy Of St John Bosco, Bootle

# Park

It was cold and dark
I go to the park
When it's night-time it goes dark
I heard a dog bark
My name is Mark
My idol is Tony Stark
I'm scared of a shark
I save a baby lark.

## Jessica O'Brien (12)
The Salesian Academy Of St John Bosco, Bootle

# Refugee

Sailing across the water
Through an endless sea
Leaving my wartorn country
Living a peaceful life
Ready to start anew.

**Luca Vincent**
The Salesian Academy Of St John Bosco, Bootle

# Acrostic Poem

**C** ure
**H** omes that are
**L** oving but
**O** verwhelmed
**E** very day.

## Chloe Williams (13)
The Salesian Academy Of St John Bosco, Bootle

# My Mum

I have three kids and a husband
I work constantly, nonstop
I pace through the day
And I'm exhausted by night

I love working with kids but they can be a handful
I know I am strong
I can do things independently
I love my childminding kids, treating them as my own

I have a good life
And wouldn't change it for the world
As well as working and being a full-time mum
I love my lazy days as some

When I haven't got my kids
I love cleaning and seeing my own mum
My mum is special to me
Without her, I don't know what I would do

I love her with all my heart
My family too
This is my message
To love your loved ones
As well as I do.

## Kacey Brown (13)
Uddingston Grammar School, Uddingston

# YOUNG WRITERS INFORMATION

We hope you have enjoyed reading this book – and that you will continue to in the coming years.

If you're a young writer who enjoys reading and creative writing, or the parent of an enthusiastic poet or story writer, do visit our website www.youngwriters.co.uk. Here you will find free competitions, workshops and games, as well as recommended reads, a poetry glossary and our blog. There's lots to keep budding writers motivated to write!

If you would like to order further copies of this book, or any of our other titles, then please give us a call or order via your online account.

Young Writers
Remus House
Coltsfoot Drive
Peterborough
PE2 9BF
(01733) 890066
info@youngwriters.co.uk

Join in the conversation!
Tips, news, giveaways and much more!

YoungWritersUK  YoungWritersCW
youngwriterscw  youngwriterscw